Henry MacArthur

Realism and Romance

And Other Essays

Henry MacArthur

Realism and Romance
And Other Essays

ISBN/EAN: 9783337007102

Printed in Europe, USA, Canada, Australia, Japan

Cover: Foto ©Thomas Meinert / pixelio.de

More available books at **www.hansebooks.com**

REALISM AND ROMANCE

AND OTHER ESSAYS

BY THE LATE

HENRY MACARTHUR

EDINBURGH: R. W. HUNTER

1897

Edinburgh: T. and A. Constable, Printers to Her Majesty

PREFACE

A strong desire having been expressed by friends and admirers of the late Mr. Henry MacArthur to obtain a permanent memorial of him, a Committee was formed to issue a selection from his writings, and this volume is the outcome of the movement.

Henry MacArthur was born at Bowfield, Howwood, Renfrewshire, on 15th April 1872, and was educated at Howwood Public School, where, according to his teacher, he was *facile princeps* and the most talented scholar of his experience. He afterwards attended Hutcheson's Grammar School, Glasgow.

He studied for the Civil Service, sat for the Boy Clerkships examination, taking first place for Scotland, began official work in the service of the Board of Lunacy, was transferred to H.M. Register House, and later to the Exchequer

Office, where he remained up till the time of his death on 24th November 1896.

In Edinburgh he took the opportunity of attending various classes at the Heriot-Watt College and the University. At the former he gained first prizes in English Literature, Political Economy, and Greek; and at the latter also first prizes for Essays in English Literature and Political Economy. He afterwards was a successful competitor for the Lord Rector's and Gray prizes for Essays on Burke and Erasmus, both of which are included in this volume.

These remarkable successes demonstrate his brilliant scholarly attainments; and the fact that all the essays were written by one so young gives undoubted proof of the possession of distinctive literary abilities, which he was constrained to exercise during his leisure time by his passionate love of learning and literature.

His brief literary career caused great expectation to be entertained of his future work by competent judges. Among these, Professor Masson writes as follows:—'I had occasion to take strong note of MacArthur, and to conceive high hopes of his future; and few things have impressed me more, or remain more sadly in my memory, than the unexpected news of his melancholy death.'

Those who knew Mr. MacArthur best agree in ascribing to him the highest personal qualities. Utterly devoid of affectation, and possessed of that saving sense of humour which kept him free from pedantry, he had a quiet but manly presence; a genuine and unaffected modesty of demeanour; a kindly, gentle nature; a thoughtfulness for others; a pure and high walk and conversation; a consuming love of what was best in literature and life, and an abiding sense of duty to himself and to his neighbours. These qualities endeared him to all who had the privilege of his society and friendship.

In the first two lines of his last poem, written surely in a prophetic moment, he penned his own epitaph :

> 'He died too soon, who knew so well to live,
>   That sword-bright spirit, in so frail a sheath.'

It only remains to explain that the essays, with one exception, were written without a view to publication, and they have been printed without editing.

The Committee desire to place on record their best thanks to the Right Honourable J. P. B. Robertson, to the Editor of the *Scots Magazine*, and to the Secretary of the Gray Trustees, for their kind permission to include the Essays on Burke, Fergusson, and Erasmus respectively. Their thanks are also due to the representatives of Mr. MacArthur for allowing them to print the other papers in the book. They must also acknowledge their indebtedness to Mr. W. L. Carrie of George Watson's College for his kindly assistance and advice in selecting the Essays.

On behalf of the Committee,

JAMES LEISHMAN, *Convener.*
DAVID WILKIE, *Secretary.*

EDINBURGH, *7th August* 1897.

CONTENTS

REALISM AND ROMANCE: THOMAS HARDY AND R. L. STEVENSON.[1]

To the outsider the world of letters seems a very placid and serene region, to enter which is to bid farewell for the time to the storms and heats and controversies which rage without its bounds. But the truth is that warfare about literary schools and methods is as incessant as our political squabbles; a change of style excites as much interest as a change of Ministry, and a critical pronouncement by one having authority as much discussion, almost, as the manifesto of a party leader. I shall first of all take note of one of these controversies — that, namely, between the realistic and romantic schools of fiction, and shall afterwards write of two living authors who may be taken as fairly representative of these two schools.

Not long ago, whenever the Secretary of a Debating Society was gravelled for lack of matter, he was wont to propound some such question as,

[1] Heriot-Watt College Literary Society, Nov. 1893.

A

'Is Novel-reading injurious?' or, 'Does History teach more than Fiction?' and the young men bent on what is oddly enough called mutual improvement never failed to rise to the bait. These ingenuous inquiries seem rather belated now; the idea that fiction has still its spurs to win is almost discarded, and on all sides the novel is recognised as the prime force in the literature of to-day.

But when Jeshurun waxed fat he kicked, and the novelists no sooner became the men of the hour than straightway they fell to fisticuffs with one another. It comes, perhaps, of taking themselves and their art a trifle too seriously. One can fancy how Scott would have lifted his eyebrows had he been asked whether he thought himself a realist or a romantic. But then of course Scott was a mere trifler, who did not understand the A B C of his art; so, at least, Mr. W. D. Howells has lately been telling us, and Mr. Howells ought to know, because he is a novelist himself, and lives in Boston. Some of us, indeed, cling foolishly to the belief that Scott was no fool, that the man could once in a while write a decent story; and one or two are audacious enough to hint that Mr. Howells's attacks on him and others of our literary idols only prove how bad a critic a very good novelist may be. But this, as the phrase goes, is a digression. Whether, then, we like it or not, the ball has been set rolling, and the battle between the two schools goes on in a very lively and spirited fashion.

What, then, are the points at issue? At the outset, I must take notice of the fact that many people attach merely a bad meaning to the term 'Realism'; it stands with them for whatever in literature is coarse, immoral, suggestive. This, let me say at once, is not the sense in which I understand the term. I cannot even see the propriety of applying the epithet at all to the writers whom people have in their eye when they think of realism and realists in that way. These writers picture man as consistently base and corrupt. They fix their eyes upon a malodorous cesspool swarming with vile creatures, and forget the blue heavens over their head, and the everlasting hills around them, and the grass under their feet. They put a pitiful fragment of man's life for the whole of it; and when they think to give us a faithful portrait, they produce merely a squinting and leering caricature. They call themselves the school of Naturalism; Animalism were perhaps the fitter term. Well, then, it seems to me that the proper criticism to pass upon such work is to say—not that it is bad because it is realistic, but —that it is not truly realistic at all. Realists they may be in intention, but not in effect. The aim of the realist should be to see life steadily, and see it whole, and these do neither. They have no sense of proportion; their vision is narrow and distorted, and what they do *not* see is vastly more important than what they do see. The true realists are such writers as Mr. Hardy for English rural life, and Mr. George Gissing for life in our great cities.

Taking realism, then, in this sense, what are the broad characteristics of the two schools? The object of the realist is to present us with a faithful transcript of the facts of life; the romantic writer, on the other hand, gives a loose rein to his fancy and follows where it leads. Realism is the home-keeping Cinderella; the romantic, in his fine disdain of the prosaic and merely common-place, tricks himself out in the oddest dresses, and swaggers over the world in search of adventures. The realist keeps to the present day; the romantic prefers the fifteenth century to the nineteenth. The pomp and circumstance of Courts, brave deeds by land and sea, the delight of battle, the spice of danger—these are to the romantic as the breath of his nostrils; the realist works with far humbler and homelier material. To the romantic we look for broad and striking effects, for stirring scenes, for hurrying, pell-mell action; under the guidance of the realist we enter a serener atmosphere, a world in which the lights are lowered and the colours are toned down.

But it may be asked, Why should these be thought of as antagonistic to one another? And to me there seems peculiar pertinence in the inquiry. The answer must be that offence has come mainly from the realistic camp. The extreme advocates of this school, taking, as I have said, their art very seriously, are inclined to look upon the rival practitioners with undisguised contempt. Mere idle dreamers, they say, and the novelist nowadays must be a very serious person, looking before and after, and striving to puzzle out the riddle of human existence. This, they proceed, is before all a scientific age, and if the novel is to hold its ground it must become scientific also. To simple souls, blissfully ignorant of science, and loving Shakespeare better than Euclid, the retort might seem easy that since we are becoming so very scientific, it might perhaps be well to leave one region free to the imagination and the fancy. Science, they would say, is no doubt a very admirable thing, and we are quite content to join in its praises so long as you do not require us to study it; but also it is apt to be rather arid and unattractive, and on the whole we fancy that we should not like the scientific novel. For my own part, I must confess that I am quite unable to attach any meaning to this conception of the novel as a scientific product. The novelist is a man ; and, try as he may, his own temper and outlook upon things will influence his view of those facts of life which he conceives it to be his business to put into fiction. That is to say, the personal equation must inevitably enter into his work. But the personal equation can have no place in science. A scientific work of art is, in short, a glaring contradiction in terms, and all that the realist means is that the novelist should depend on observation rather than on imagination, and that he should be a philosopher as well as a story-teller.

On the other side, the romantic advocates have not been slow to hit back. A novel, they say, is meant to give pleasure, to lift us out of ourselves, to make us forget our daily cares and problems and worries. And this it will hardly do if it concerns itself with those very cares and problems and worries from which we wish to escape. Here, again, the extremists seem to me in error. A cynic might rejoin that, as a matter of fact, people *do* take pleasure in hearing of the worries of other people, and that this pleasure may even make them forget their own. But this would be taking very low ground indeed. The question seems to turn on what we mean by giving pleasure. When the advocate of romance denies that realistic novels give pleasure, what he has in his mind is that the realist has commonly a somewhat sombre view of life, and that he has a preference for unhappy endings. But then are we to say that the *Merchant of Venice* gives pleasure, and that *Hamlet* does not; or that *Guy Mannering* gives pleasure, and not *The Bride of Lammermoor?* The truth is, that this squeamish horror of unhappy endings has played havoc with many a promising novel and play. Surely a novel may give pleasure of a very high order although it ends not with the merry jingling of the marriage-bells, but with the harsh and discordant accents of tragedy, and although from its last page there should steal a perfume more potent than that of orange-flowers.

And when the advocates of romance go on to ridicule the method of the realist they seem not less in error. 'A transcript of the facts of life,' they say; there needs no genius for that, only a note-book and a lead-pencil. This sounds plausible, but is radically unjust. A note-book and a lead-pencil, although very harmless and useful articles (as Serjeant Buzfuz said of the warming-pan), can by no means be considered as the whole outfit of the realistic writer. He must have the eye to see, the power of selection, arrangement, and combination, the faculty of separating the trivial from the essential. And in the conduct of the story, the fact that he must aim at keeping within the limits of the possible and normal course of things does not make imagination and dramatic insight unnecessary. This is so obvious that one is almost ashamed to call attention to it, but it is a point often missed or ignored in diatribes against the realistic school.

We may now have some notion of how the case stands between the two schools. The distinguishing marks of the realistic school may be summed up thus:—(1) That it keeps to the present day, and aims at keeping within the limits of the possible. (2) That it depends for its interest on character rather than on incident. (3) That in its manner and choice of subjects it is bold and unconventional; and that it deals freely with certain aspects of life hitherto left untouched or very gingerly handled. (4) That it aims at painting real men and women, not ideal men and women.

We have also seen reason to dissent from the extreme views on either side. But what is to be our final judgment on the two schools. Well, in the first place, I dislike the idea of carrying into a thing so soft, fluid, and many-hued as literature the sharp distinctions imperatively called for by the requirements of science. And, in the second place, I think that a wide catholicity of taste is the truest wisdom in literature. The House Beautiful of Art has many mansions, and to-day we may take our ease in one of them, and to-morrow sit under the porch or cross the threshold of another. Sectarianism in literature is as wrong and mischievous as sectarianism in religion, and alas! it is almost as common. And so of these two schools we should not let our preconceived theories prevent us from taking the best that each has to offer us. In this we shall have the sanction of the best writers of either school, for I know that Mr. Stevenson admires Mr. Hardy, and I make no doubt that Mr. Hardy enjoys his *Treasure Island* like the rest of us.

'Tis a wide world, my masters, and this rude jostling and loud decrying are as needless as they are unseemly. There is room for both; room for the writer who merely aims at telling a story, as for the more ambitious attempt to interpret in fiction the facts of life; room even for Mr. Howells and what I may call the Needy Knife-Grinder Novelist, who say to us: 'Story, Lord bless you, sir, we've none to tell.'

It is true, no doubt, that the vogue is passing more and more to the realistic novel; the tone and temper of the age are all on its side. As

Sainte-Beuve, the great French critic, has put it : 'The ideal has ceased ; the lyric vein has dried up ; the new men are cured of lyricism and the ideal ; a severe and pitiless truth has made its entry, as the last word of experience, even into art itself.' But with all this the romantic has still its charm and its fascination for us ; the Dumas and Scotts and Stevensons have still their beneficent part to play. To soothe the tired brain and calm the overstrained nerves, to carry us into a world where they pass the time carelessly as they did in the golden age, to delight our eyes and senses with gallant and gorgeous pageants, to appeal to that healthy feeling for action and deeds of high prowess, for all that is heroic in man and lovely in woman—these are no mean achievements, and so long as human nature is what it is, the novel which does this will not wholly lose its dominion over men's minds.

And so, having tried to do justice to both schools, and to vindicate each in turn from the strictures of its opponents, let me conclude this part of my subject with the just and eloquent words of Mr. Walter Pater—words not written, I may explain, with reference to this particular controversy. 'The legitimate contention,' says he, 'is not that of one age or school of literary art against another, but of all successive schools alike against the stupidity which is dead to the substance and the vulgarity which is dead to form.'

Mr. Thomas Hardy, whom I take as representing the dominant school of Realism, is, by the general consent of competent critics, recognised as one, and not the least, of that chosen band with whom the immediate future of English fiction rests. Indeed, till very lately, Mr. Hardy was a greater favourite with the critics than with the public ; and even yet one could name writers, with not a tenth part of his power, who yet count many more readers than he. But honest work makes its way in the end, and the decisive success of his latest novel is a thing for all lovers of good literature to rejoice in. Mr. Hardy may now be said to have fairly won the public ear, and it will be strange if he does not keep it.

The field in which Mr. Hardy has chosen to work is the south-western corner of England, what in the days of the Saxons was known as Wessex. All his best work deals with the lives of very humble and obscure persons in that district. Casterbridge is Mr. Hardy's Thrums. He knows the country like a book, and we feel that the rustic figures who cross his pages are drawn direct from the life. In his uncompromising realism he does not shrink from what sometimes seems a prosaic and wearisome detail, and it is not his fault if readers do not rise from his books with some notion of what country life in England is like. It is not always a pleasant picture, that which he sets before us, for Mr. Hardy has too austere an idea of the novelist's function to palter with his art for the sake of casting an ideal glamour over his rustics and their ways. He paints them as they are, with their quaint, old-world ways, their dense ignorance, their somewhat low moral tone. Absolute truth, absolute sincerity—these are the notes of his work. His books give the lie direct to the theory that the novelist in order to interest us must go far afield for his subjects. Round the lives of these simple peasants Mr. Hardy weaves his striking stories of love and passion and suffering. His tales stand out from the ruck of novels by reason of their sympathetic realism, for, in literature, knowledge enters ever by the door of sympathy. 'What is called poetic insight'—so writes Nathaniel Hawthorne—'What is called poetic insight is the power of discerning in this sphere of strangely mixed elements the beauty and the majesty which are compelled to assume a garb so sordid.' A large measure of this insight has been granted to Mr. Hardy, and so there passes into his pages the pathos of ill-requited toil, of weary limbs and aching backs and stunted minds. This simple rural life, with its weary round of duties, its constant and monotonous toil, its grey uniformity of colour, might have seemed to us poor, petty, and uninteresting enough in all conscience, but there comes a man with the eye of the artist, and lo! the elements of romance and tragedy are here also. And this is none other than the supreme triumph of the realist.

Mr. Hardy is often spoken of as if he were above all a humorist, but that, to my mind, is a fundamentally false conception of the man. Only in his first two books (for *Desperate Remedies*, his 'prentice work, hardly counts)—only, I say, in *Under the Greenwood Tree* and *Far from the Madding Crowd* does his humour flow fresh and clear. That charming idyll of country life, *Under the Greenwood Tree*, though far from being Mr. Hardy's greatest book, is perhaps the most pleasant, certainly it is the most genial. Full of truth and full of sunlight, it shows Mr. Hardy in his lightest and most pleasing vein. Not again was he to do anything so admirably humorous and genial as this. In his next book, *Far from the Madding Crowd*, admirably humorous as it is in parts, we already note a more reflective and a more sombre tone. And as novel has followed novel this sadder mood has grown upon Mr. Hardy till in *Tess* he has given us a novel wholly tragic in its interest, as *Under the Greenwood Tree* is wholly idyllic. With the growth of this sombre habit of mind his humour has changed its colour, and often sounds like bitter irony. One misses, too, in his work that happy lightness of touch which is all but indispensable to the humorist.

It is hardly, then, in Mr. Hardy's humour that I should seek the key to his strength. Nor has he a great command over the softer sentiments, or a great power of pure pathos. But in sheer tragic power he has scarcely an equal among living writers. Mr. Hardy, on the higher plane where pathos, as it were, is swallowed up and transcended by tragedy, puts forth his full strength. His greatest books, *The Return of the Native*, *The Mayor of Casterbridge*, *Tess of the D'Urbervilles*, are all cast in a tragic mould: his best-drawn characters are those whose ends are tragic, whose lot it is to suffer and die. Michael Henchard, 'the Mayor of Casterbridge,' seems to me Mr. Hardy's best bit of portraiture; strength and subtlety go together in the handling. Here at last in fiction we have a man wholly alive, wholly virile. Only genius could have drawn with so firm a hand and so rare a skill the portrait of this man—a man passionate,

coarse-grained, wrong-headed, but at bottom
neither ignoble nor ungenerous. He plays his
hand in so honest and downright a way that our
sympathies go to him almost against our judgment,
and knowing him to be in the wrong, it is yet
not without regret that we see him beaten and
foiled at every point in the game. And when,
stripped of fortune and the love of friends, he turns
his back on Casterbridge, and seeks the country
to die, our imagination follows with infinite pity
the despairing outcast. Few things in fiction
strike a deeper chord than that strange document,
Michael Henchard's Will.

> 'That Elizabeth-Jane Farfrae be not told of
> my death, or made to grieve on account
> of me.
>
> '& that I be not bury'd in consecrated ground.
>
> '& that no sexton be asked to toll the bell.
>
> '& that nobody is wished to see my dead body.
>
> '& that no murners walk behind me at my
> funeral.
>
> '& that no flours be planted on my grave.
>
> '& that no man remember me.
>
> 'To this I put my name.'

On this what comment is possible save that of
Elizabeth-Jane? 'O Donald,' she said at last,
'what bitterness lies there!'

In *The Return of the Native* there are passages

of equal intensity and power ; as, for example, the chapter entitled 'The Closed Door,' or again, that great scene between Clym and Eustacia when he discovers the truth about his mother's death. From his first bitterly ironical words, 'It seems my wife is not well,' his agonised cry, 'Eustacia, you have held my happiness in the hollow of your hand, and like a devil you have dashed it down,' the dialogue is almost intolerable in its power. Readers of *Far from the Madding Crowd* will hardly have forgotten the description of Fanny Robin crawling painfully to the workhouse to die, or the passionate scene between Sergeant Troy and Bathsheba over her coffin. And *Tess of the D'Urbervilles* is from beginning to end pitched in a tragic key.

Mr. Hardy is said to be no great favourite with the young ladies of the circulating library, who sometimes annotate the margins of his books with 'I think Mr. Hardy is a horrid man!' 'I am sure Bathsheba would have done no such thing,' and other comments of that profound and enlightening character. The reasons for this extreme disfavour are not far to seek. Mr. Hardy does not allow sentiment to run riot through his pages, and Mr. Mudie's young ladies get, rightly or wrongly, the name of dearly loving that peculiarly feminine luxury known as a 'good cry.' His books may be read dry-eyed, for, as I have said, he touches springs of feeling which lie too deep for tears. But there is more—and worse—behind. His view of the fair sex is curiously consistent, and, as some think, over-cynical. When he says of Eustacia Vye that she 'had the passions and instincts which make a model goddess, that is, those which make not quite a model woman,' he really passes judgment on nearly all his heroines— Tess excepted. 'Nearly every one of the ladies,' says a critic, 'practically propose to one man, two run after him to do so, and one of them then marries another.' We hear a great deal now of woman's rights: well, Mr. Hardy is a consistent advocate of the greatest of these rights, that of changing her mind with or without cause assigned. The strange thing is that they do not seem grateful to him for it. Most of his heroines have several wooers—three, I have calculated, is the average number. This, of course, is quite in accordance with the English tradition, but their peculiarity is that they seem to experience a distracting difficulty in choosing between them. Mr. Hardy seems to revel in painting their whims, their caprices, their delightful vanity, their involuntary cruelty. Readers accustomed to the bread-and-butter misses of English fiction must feel sorely at a loss to know what to make of these charmingly unconventional creations, these fair maidens with whom it is always leap-year. Perhaps we are to take it as a sign that in fiction, as in real life, women are beginning to abandon that merely passive *rôle* with which they were once content. Whether Mr. Hardy's view is the right one is a point which I do not feel competent to decide. I am content to own that I find them very good company, and to note the dictum of Mr. J. M. Barrie, who is certainly neither a cynic nor a woman-hater. 'Mr. Hardy's women,' says Mr. Barrie, 'are the most interesting in their unconventionality, the most charming in their womanliness, and the most subtly drawn, with the exception of Mr. Meredith's, that this generation of novelists has given us.' That is handsomely said, and for me it is conclusive.

In the matter of style, Mr. Hardy can barely be said to rank with the highest. He has neither the erratic brilliance of Mr. Meredith nor the subtle charm of Mr. Stevenson. His style is slow-footed ; it lacks alertness and vivacity. He is far from being a flawless writer ; crudities of phrase abound ; his diction is sometimes distressingly scientific ; his touch often ineffectual and fumbling. Often, indeed, he strikes out a profound aphorism, but the crispness and polish of epigram are usually lacking. At best his style may be described as a *useful* one. At times, however, one comes upon a passage which arrests us by its felicity; as, for example, his description of Eustacia Vye: 'To see her hair was to fancy that a whole winter night did not contain darkness enough to form its shadow; it closed over her forehead like nightfall extinguishing the western glow. . . . She had Pagan eyes, full of nocturnal mysteries. . . . Her presence brought memories of such things as Bourbon roses, rubies, and tropical midnights; her moods recalled lotus-eaters and the march in *Athalie*; her motions, the ebb and flow of the sea; her voice, the viola.' Such passages show that behind the realist in Mr. Hardy there is the poet; and indeed a fine imaginativeness runs like a thread of gold through the homespun texture of his work. He has the poet's fine feeling, too, for the external world; the man has clearly communed with Nature as a lover, although his defects of style prevent him from adequately rendering her moods, and what he gives us is a photograph rather than a picture. This is specially noticeable in *The Return of the Native*, in which Egdon Heath is the dark background of a sombre drama. When the end is coming amid storm, darkness, and spiritual tempest, this is how Mr. Hardy writes: 'The gloom of the night was funereal; all nature seemed clothed in crape. . . . It was a night which led the traveller's thoughts instinctively to dwell on nocturnal scenes of disaster in the chronicles of the world, on all that is terrible and dark in history and legend—the last plague of Egypt, the destruction of Sennacherib's host, the Agony in Gethsemane.' This is truly, in the words of Keats, to

> 'behold upon the night's starred face
> Huge cloudy symbols of a high romance.'

The sombre hue of that last picture reflects what one fancies is Mr. Hardy's habitual mood. His books represent that reaction against a hollow and unreal optimism which has set in so strongly in our day. His tone is deeply tinged with pessimism ; the man seems haunted by an abiding sense of what he finely calls 'the ironical sequence of things.' No sooner do we set the cup of happiness to our lips than it is dashed from our hands, or turns to poison in the drinking. He perpetually recurs to this theme, and dwells upon it with what I must call a morbid insistence. 'When she plodded on in the shade of the hedge, silently thinking, she had the hard half-apathetic expression of one who deems anything possible at the hands of Time and Chance, except, perhaps, fair-play.' — 'Except, perhaps, fair-play,' how profoundly significant that touch is of Mr. Hardy's temper! The vast and terrible irony of Fate, 'the dust and ashes of things, the cruelty of lust and the fragility of love': it is on these that his mind fixes itself with a painful intensity. One can imagine him saying with the blind Gloucester in *King Lear*:—

> 'As flies to wanton boys, so are we to the gods :
> They kill us for their sport.'

Sometimes he turns it into a jest, but his laughter has a hard and bitter ring. He calls *The Hand of Ethelberta* a 'Comedy in Chapters'; to me the story seems more ghastly than his direst tragedies. There are things for which one cannot find it in one's heart to forgive even one's favourite authors, and the marriage of Ethelberta to Lord Mountclere, like the nagging of Colonel Newcome by his son's mother-in-law, is one of these. *Tess of the D'Urbervilles* works in us that 'honest sadness which comes of a logical and inevitable tragedy'; *The Hand of Ethelberta* merely exasperates us, and sets our teeth on edge, and surely it can never be the province of good art to do that. Mr. Hardy should abjure tragi-comedy; he has better stuff in him than to decline upon Thackeray's worst manner. The sense of revolt against intolerable injustice is strongly marked in *Tess*, so that it reads like a tremendous indictment of the whole order of the Universe. On this book let me quote the verdict of Mr. William Watson: 'Powerful and strange in design, splendid and terrible in execution, this story brands itself upon the mind as with the touch of incandescent iron.' And again : '*Tess* must take its place among the great tragedies, to have read which is to have enlarged the boundaries of one's intellectual and emotional experience.' In that I join heartily, yet I must repeat that there is something morbid and turbid in this spirit of vain and impotent revolt, something very far removed from the even and equable serenity of the artist. Shakespeare must have felt like this when, with the world darkened around him, he sat down to write his great tragedies. But with him the mood passed, and one would like to think that Mr. Hardy also will yet shake himself free from this malignant influence. He has given us his *Lear* : when are we to see his *Winter's Tale*? Great things may yet be hoped from a writer still in the prime of life, who has already added so much to the strength and richness of contemporary fiction. To Mr. Hardy, then, belongs in an eminent degree that supreme merit which Mr. Swinburne, in a magnificent phrase, once ascribed to Byron — 'the

imperishable excellence of sincerity and strength.'
Sincerity and strength — these are indeed imperishable; and hence of Mr. Hardy we may
safely predict that his fame will be stable and
enduring.

ROBERT LOUIS STEVENSON

That very pleasing writer, the author of *Obiter
Dicta* and *Res Judicatae*, speaks somewhere of
the 'Clan Stevenson.'   Mr. Birrell refers, of
course, to those who have come under the spell
of Mr. Stevenson's fascinating personality, who
have been won by the engaging charm of his
style: this is the Clan Stevenson, and of this
clan I delight to think myself a humble member.
Charles Lamb, you remember, talks of certain
writers whose names, he says, 'carry a perfume
in the mention': his own name is now one of
these; Mr. Stevenson's, I think, is another.   Like
Lamb, he speaks to his readers as to friends and
familiars; an egoist (in the good sense) of the
first water, he abounds in confidences; he draws
one by his gracious and winning worldliness no
less than by the sure perfection of his style.   He
is profoundly interested in himself, and so he
never fails to interest us.   In the presence of
work so captivating as his, so exquisite in its

literary quality, one feels inclined to strike one's colours and to abdicate the critical function.

The aroma and savour of style—this it is which makes Mr. Stevenson's books so uniformly delightful to the literary epicure. There is no alchemy like that of style; it transmutes into gold whatever it touches. Think of the verse of Shakespeare, that wave of sound breaking into a thousand clear ripples of melody, of the interwoven harmonies of Milton, or again, of the unadorned but terribly effective style of Swift, a style which makes us think of a woodman hewing down trees with a mighty swing of the arm: so great is the power, so various the quality of style in literature!

And what are we to say of Mr. Stevenson's style? Hasty readers praise it for its qualities of simplicity and straightforwardness. But simple Mr. Stevenson's style is not; on the contrary, he is one of the most patient, cunning, and dexterous artificers in English prose. Mr. Hardy uses language as a good workman uses his tools; Mr. Stevenson, it has been well said, plays upon words as if they were a musical instrument. His description of the old beggar in *Across the Plains* fits himself like a glove: 'What took him was a richness in the speech; he loved the exotic, the unexpected word; the moving cadence of a phrase; a vague sense of emotion (about nothing) in the very letters of the alphabet: the romance of language.' The artfulness of his diction is something to marvel at; the language grows plastic at his touch; he moulds it to his liking. So severely fastidious is his taste, that you may search his books from cover to cover without lighting upon a single slovenly or slipshod phrase. He is the first of the literary exquisites, the Keats of English prose; hackneyed forms of speech he shuns as he would the pestilence; with him distinction is a matter of course. This sedulous avoidance of the commonplace has of course its dangers. A writer who is never content to say things as other people say them, must sometimes pay the penalty by saying them worse; his style is apt to degenerate into mannerism. Mannerisms Mr. Stevenson no doubt has; in particular, he is rather too fond of French idioms; but nine times out of ten he fairly hits the bull's-eye. On his own confession, we can hardly grant him the praise of originality; he has borrowed much from Elizabethan writers, a fact which explains the somewhat archaic cast of his diction. The grand style he does not pretend to. In place of the flushed and magnificent rhetoric of Milton and Jeremy Taylor, he gives us a richly-wrought mosaic of dainty words and phrases. Occasionally he affects a somewhat mincing gait; he is overmuch concerned to cut his capers and play his pretty tricks when we should prefer to see him break into a downright gallop. As an example of his style at its best, I quote a very beautiful and very touching passage on Scotland and Edinburgh. Mark the fine felicity of phrase, and the melodious cadence of the evolution :—

'There is no special loveliness in that grey country, with its rainy, sea-beat archipelago; its fields of dark mountains; its unsightly places black with coal; its treeless, sour, unfriendly-looking corn-lands; its quaint grey, castled city, where the bells clash of a Sunday and the winds squall and the salt showers fly and beat. I do not even know if I desire to live there; but let me hear in some far land a kindred voice sing out, "Oh why left I my hame?" and it seems at once as if no beauty under the kind heavens, and no society of the wise and good, can repay me for my absence from my country. And though I think I would rather die elsewhere, yet in my heart of hearts I long to be buried among good Scots clods. . . . When I forget thee, Auld Reekie, may my right hand forget its cunning.' 'The happiest lot on earth,' he proceeds, 'is to be born a Scotsman. You must pay for it in many ways,

as for all other advantages on earth. You have to
learn the paraphrases and the Shorter Catechism ;
you generally take to drink ; your youth, as far
as I can learn, is a time of louder war against
society, of more outcry and tears and turmoil,
than if you had been born, for instance, in England. But somehow life is warmer and closer ;
the lights of home shine softer on the rainy
street; the very names endeared in verse and
music cling nearer round our heart.'

But it is time to turn to Mr. Stevenson's
romances. A nice sense for the subtleties of
style is not perhaps very widely diffused, and it
was a fortunate day for Mr. Stevenson when it
occurred to him to enter into competition with
the purveyors of books for boys. *Treasure Island*,
the first-fruit of this resolve, is in its way a
classic. 'There should be nothing so much a
man's business as his amusements,' says Mr.
Stevenson ; and certainly he at any rate is always
dead in earnest in his play. The narrative is set
down with so convincing an air of reality that it
almost imposes on our senses. If Mr. Hardy
often gives us the romance of realism, Mr.
Stevenson succeeds admirably in giving us the
realism of romance. Nor is the interest of
Treasure Island solely that of sensational incident.
The characters are graphically presented with

true dramatic genius. Who that has read the book can forget John Silver, that smooth-spoken and plausible villain? There is a curious pathetic touch in the marooned sailor who dreamt of 'cheese—toasted chiefly—and I awoke, and here I were.' And that eerie tapping of the blind man's stick along the frosty road long haunts the reader's memory.

Kidnapped takes even higher rank as a story. The fight in the round-house, the flight across the moor, the quarrel on the heather, are all in Mr. Stevenson's happiest manner. But the triumph of the book is Alan Breck, a creation worthy of the hand of Scott himself. Alan's dash and gallantry are irresistible, and we smile indulgently at his unconscionable vanity. Mr. Stevenson has committed a crime past forgiveness in making Alan play second fiddle to Mr. David Balfour of Shaws in the sequel to *Kidnapped*, published the other day. 'It is the lot of sequels to disappoint,' says Mr. Stevenson, and *Catriona* is hardly an exception to the rule. The story drags at the outset; Mr. Stevenson seems to lose himself in the wilderness of the Appin murder. We are not so much interested as he seems to be in the ins and outs of that case, and the story of legal chicanery and *finesse*, artfully as it is told, is pale and thin after the breadth and daring of

Treasure Island and *Kidnapped*. But David Balfour, with his dour honesty and his good conceit of himself, is admirable; and the love-story of the youthful pair is told with Mr. Stevenson's happiest art. Mr. Stevenson seems in this book to have laid himself out to dispose once for all of the reproach that he cannot paint a woman. Ladies, indeed, have no business in books for boys; Jack and Tom may submit to their intrusion just as they submit to being kissed by their sisters, but they do not like it all the same. But *Catriona* is not a boy's book, and in it Mr. Stevenson has given us two charming women—Catriona herself, with her simplicity, her courage, her quick temper, her picturesque speech, and Miss Barbara Grant, with her arch and audacious wit, her biting tongue, her sterling soundness of heart. The critics, to my thinking, have been unduly hard on *The Black Arrow*, though, perhaps, it is not one of Mr. Stevenson's great triumphs. *The Wrecker*, one of his latest books, is a wonderfully picturesque romance, full of life and glowing with colour; 'full,' in his own words, 'of details of our barbaric manners and unstable morals; full of the need and lust of money, so that there is scarce a page in which the dollars do not jingle; full of the unrest and movement of our century, so that the reader is hurried from place to place, and sea to sea, and the book is less a romance than a panorama—in the end as blood-bespattered as an epic.' But skill seems lacking in its construction ; he is terribly long of coming to the point. The story hangs so badly together, that it resembles more a series of picturesque incidents than a coherent romance. *Prince Otto* strikes me as an experiment, not wholly successful, in the manner of Mr. George Meredith.

The Master of Ballantrae, and some of Mr. Stevenson's short stories, I have left to the last, because they show the darker and grimmer side of his genius. In *The Master of Ballantrae* the atmosphere is leaden. The two brothers are admirably contrasted, and the grim story of their hates and loves is told with consummate address. The same love for the grim and the weird shows forth in many of Mr. Stevenson's shorter tales, in *Jekyll and Hyde*, that fine allegory of the double life, for example, and in that little masterpiece, *Thrawn Janet*. When Mr. Stevenson ventures thus boldly into the region of the supernatural, Hawthorne rather than Scott, I should fancy, is his master ; and indeed he could have no better guide. No writer known to me uses the supernatural with so fine a tact as Hawthorne, so just a perception of the part it can be made to play in fiction ; in that shadowy borderland between the natural and supernatural he walks with a firm and sure footing. Mr. Stevenson has taken pattern by Hawthorne with the happiest results.

Mr. Stevenson is sometimes hailed as the successor of Scott. But a careful comparison of their work hardly bears out the resemblance. On the one hand, Mr. Stevenson has not the great master's wonderful richness, variety, and inexhaustible fertility ; his inventive genius is of a lower order, his romance of a commoner quality. On the other hand, Scott was an inveterate sloven, and his incredible carelessness grievously impairs the artistic quality of his work. Scott, in short, was a great novelist ; Mr. Stevenson is an exquisite artist. The rich and lavish prodigality of Scott is quite foreign to Mr. Stevenson's nature; but in all that concerns the *technique* of his art, in style, in symmetry, in the sense of proportion, he is immeasurably Scott's superior.

One word in conclusion. There are those among us who profess a fine contempt for all that is being done by writers who have the misfortune not yet to be dead. And perhaps to all of us there come times when we fancy we could be richly content with the goodly heritage of the past, and content to let the stream of contemporary literature flow by us unheeded. But

surely this is a shallow view to take in the face
of work so strong and powerful as Mr. Hardy's,
so delicate and exquisite as Mr. Stevenson's. I
cannot think that when Time has done his
winnowing and sifting work, we shall feel reason
to be ashamed of having sat under the greenwood tree with Mr. Hardy, of having voyaged
with Mr. Stevenson in search of Treasure Island.
And from another point of view, the thought is
an inspiring one, that these 'realms of gold' are
indeed boundless, that Art has still its unexplored
regions, its undiscovered countries, and that to
find a New World there needs only a new
Columbus.

THE WRITINGS OF EDMUND BURKE [1]

'Nitor in adversum' [2]

AMONG English statesmen, Edmund Burke holds a unique place. The figure of Chatham is a more dazzling and imposing one than that of Burke; his eloquence burns with a finer and brighter flame; the few ringing phrases of his astounding oratory which have descended to us still seem, after the lapse of more than a century, to thrill our senses as Burke's rarely does. To the younger Pitt, again, there belongs the prestige of those long years during which he held the post of First Minister, and guided with a masterly hand the ship of state. Burke held office for but a few months, and then in a subordinate situation. On the other hand, he stands in contrast to purely speculative writers on politics, such as Locke; for although he never attained to high official rank, he was, during the greater part of his life, in the

---

[1] Lord Rector's Prize Essay, Edinburgh University, 1894.

[2] ' "Nitor in adversum" is the motto for a man like me.'— Burke's *Letter to a Noble Lord*.

C

very thick of the parliamentary fight, and from him his party took its ideas and drew its inspiration. Burke's peculiarity is that he combined with the minutest knowledge of what may be called the *technique* of politics a greater reach of mind, a speculative grasp, firmer and surer than that possessed by any other writer so absorbed as he was in actual political warfare. The union of these qualities is, indeed, rare. One of the acutest and most brilliant of critics—the late Walter Bagehot—once remarked of political economy that the theory of business leads a life of obstruction because the theorists do not see the business, and the men of business will not reason out the theories; and this excellent dictum is capable of a wider application to the whole field of politics. The men of detail and routine are often singularly incapable of taking a broad and philosophic view of things. Immersed in detail and routine, they have neither time nor aptitude for ascending to first principles;—in the popular phrase, they cannot see the wood for the trees. On the other hand, the philosophers who are philosophers only, who contemplate politics from an ideal altitude, are hampered by their lack of knowledge of the actual conditions of political life; in Burke's striking phrase, they do not know the map of the country; and so their work, excellent and suggestive as it sometimes is, remains, and must remain, rather vague and nebulous, too much 'in the air,' academic and unpractical.   It would be unjust to call the younger Pitt a man of detail and routine, yet it has been remarked that in his case remarkable administrative powers went hand in hand with a singular poverty of original thought; while his great rival Fox was even ostentatiously ignorant of some of the rudiments of political science.   In Burke alone is the union of the philosopher and the practical politician complete.

This, however, is only one of the contrasts which meet us in the intellect of Burke.   When we are told that a man is a philosopher, we naturally open his books, expecting to find in them a philosophic calm, an equable serenity.   But Burke is an enthusiast as well as a philosopher; in M. Taine's words, 'To all those powers of mind which constitute a man of system he added all those energies of heart which constitute an enthusiast.'[1]   What strikes one in him is that the singular caution of his reasoning, with its firm root in concrete facts, is united with an almost unexampled fervour in exposition.   In hardly any other writer do we find this union of the declamatory powers of the orator with the specu-

[1] *History of English Literature*, Book III. ch. iii.

lative powers of the philosopher.   Light and heat
do not usually go together.

Mr. Buckle has called attention to a third
contrast in Burke's intellectual constitution.
What appears to him most remarkable in Burke's
method is the 'singular sobriety with which he
employed his extraordinary acquirements.   During the best part of his life, his political principles,
so far from being speculative, were altogether
practical.   This is particularly striking because
he had every temptation to adopt an opposite
course.   He possessed materials for generalisa-
tion far more ample than any politician of his
time, and he had a mind eminently prone to take
large views.   On many occasions, and indeed
whenever an opportunity offered, he showed his
capacity as an original and speculative thinker.
But the moment he set foot on political ground
he changed his method. . . . We had no doubt
other statesmen before him who denied the
validity of general principles in politics ; but
their denial was only the happy guess of ignorance, and they rejected theories which they had
never taken the pains to study.   Burke rejected
them because he knew them.'   Every careful
student of Burke must recognise the truth of this
characterisation ; and it is most important to put
it prominently forward, for it is hardly too much

to say that it supplies the key to the essential unity of Burke's action in the great problems which engaged his attention.   In his very first political publication, we find him avowing his contempt for abstract logic as applied to politics ; and his hatred of the French Revolution sprang largely from the fact that it was an attempt to realise in practice a system of politics based on that abstract method of reasoning which he despised and distrusted.

With endowments so various and so splendid, one need not wonder that Burke impressed himself on his contemporaries as the first man of his time, or that his praises should since have been sung by critic after critic.   The verdict of contemporaries is often set aside with disdain by their successors.   But Burke's fame has known no ebb.   Men agreeing in nothing else, some of them differing widely from him, have joined in eulogising Burke.   Johnson, Hazlitt, Wordsworth, Coleridge, Buckle, Arnold, Morley have, each in his own way, given to Burke the tribute of a generous admiration.   The fastidious taste of Arnold one might have expected to be repelled by the vehemence of Burke, and by his Asiatic diction ; but the apostle of 'sweetness and light' is conquered by him, edits him, and strives to increase his audience.   Burke's last years were spent in a gigantic struggle with the French Revolution : to Mr. John Morley, one of the most brilliant apologists for that Revolution, we owe the ablest and most sympathetic study of Burke. A verdict so unanimous from a jury so unexceptionable can hardly, one thinks, be cavilled against ; and Burke's place among the Immortals seems already assured.

The characteristics of Burke's oratory have been so often described that it seems hopeless to add anything new on the subject. But after all, nothing so pregnant has been said of it as the illuminating phrase of Goldsmith. 'He winds,' said Goldsmith, 'into his subject like a serpent.' This describes with a vivid exactness the peculiar character of Burke's oratory, that circuitous method of approach which produces on the unthinking hearer the impression that Burke is going out of his way, that he will never reach his goal, and so he betakes himself to dinner. Indeed nothing more unsuited for a popular audience can well be conceived than Burke's style of oratory. Eloquent commonplace, the quick cut-and-thrust of party invective, smart personalities, speech going straight to its mark like an arrow — these are what the average politician, with his eye on the division lobby, hungers after. What was he to make of an

orator to whom politics was not a game, and the
House of Commons something other than the
'best club in England'?   The squires and
merchants who surrounded Burke solved the
problem in their own way, and went to sleep
or to dinner when the greatest genius of his time
rose to his feet.   The profundity of his thought,
the copiousness of his diction, his passion and
want of measure, his highly ornate style, simply
wearied and perplexed his hearers.   It appears,
too, that he had no external advantages, that his
voice was harsh and unmusical, his figure uncouth, his gestures clumsy and awkward.   The
whirligig of Time, however, brings in its revenges,
and the speeches which were listened to with
hardly concealed impatience now rank among
the masterpieces of English literature, and are
found to be positively the only specimens of
Parliamentary oratory which may be studied with
profit and delight.

Burke, however, is not only an orator; he is a
writer of surpassing merit.   But there is astonishingly little difference between the style of his
oratory and that of his writings; his pamphlets
might almost pass for speeches, his speeches for
pamphlets, which is, perhaps, as much as to say
that he has hardly caught the right tone for either.
He ranks among the masters of English prose;

some critics would even accord him the very highest place. Dryden is said to have been his model, and one can readily believe that with his fine and just sense in literary matters Burke would have a high regard for the writer of the most business-like prose which English literature can show till we come to Addison and Swift. But, in truth, the resemblance between Dryden and Burke is hardly apparent even to the most careful and critical research. Dryden's prose has the easy grace, the indefinable charm, of cultured conversation ; from affectation and artifice it is absolutely free. Compared with Dryden, Burke is mechanical and artificial. His merits are quite different from those of Glorious John. He comes far closer to Jeremy Taylor and the Milton of the *Areopagitica*—those masters of flushed and magnificent rhetoric—than to writers of the conversational order of prose, like Dryden and Addison. Amplitude and splendour, pomp of diction, sonorousness, solidity, massiveness—these are the epithets that rise to our lips as we read his pages. To those imbued with the classic spirit, loving that 'comely order' which Mr. Pater[1] has defined as the note of the classic temper, Burke's effects must appear violent,

---

[1] *Appreciations: Essay on the Terms 'Classical' and 'Romantic.'*

exaggerated, sometimes grotesque. The charm which the classic writers never fail to throw round their subjects one misses in Burke; his taste, also, one need scarcely say, was far from faultless. He paints with strong, sometimes even glaring, colours, on an immense canvas. But if his style sometimes suffers from over-ornamentation, at least the jewels are real and massive, not tinsel and pasteboard. One can readily understand why, to the French taste, he should appear an eloquent barbarian—like Shakespeare.[1] Alertness, vivacity, lucidity, charm, sparkle—these are what the French ask for, and Burke has not these to give. It is true that he usually sets out with a great show of order and rigour. But the stream of his thought is too full to be restrained within artificial barriers; soon it overflows its banks, and the flood breaks forth, grand and imposing, indeed, but troubled and turbid, not clear, and pure and sparkling. The evolution of his sentences is occasionally rather slow and cumbrous; and the majestic harmony of rhythm and cadence with which the prose of the very greatest masters falls on our ears we rarely hear from him. But it would be absurd to apply to Burke the rules and tests of the literary purist. The heated atmosphere

---

[1] M. Taine gives to Burke hardly one-quarter of the space he devotes to Macaulay.

of politics is not favourable to the cultivation of the literary graces. And Burke's prose, despite its somewhat slow-footed movement, its want of modulation, has an amazing richness and an un-flagging energy. One might almost say that the raw material of poetry lies in his writings; by his dazzling succession of images, his profusion of metaphor, Burke almost touches poetry, although he had not, one feels, the finely attuned ear of the born poet. He has the enthusiasm of the poet also; and his intellectual strenuousness and sincerity set him very far apart from the mere exquisites of literature, from those who do not greatly care what they say, so that it be well and tunefully said.

Johnson thought meanly of Burke's humour, and most critics will agree with the sage of Bolt Court. It is undeniable that the great orator lacked the light and deft touch of the born humor-ist. If it be true, as Edmond Schérer has con-tended,[1] that the typical humorist is a man of a rather sceptical bias, who sits at his ease in the stalls of the theatre of life, then we have an easy explanation of Burke's lack of humour. For, in truth, his temperament was just the reverse of this. His nature was ardent, vehement, impetu-

---

[1] *Études critiques sur la Littérature contemporaine*, t. vi. : *Laurence Sterne.*

ous : he took life and its issues with an habitual seriousness.   His style, rich, weighty, massive, does not lend itself to the archness, the grace, the *naïveté* of which such writers as Sterne and Goldsmith possess the secret.   But if his want of humour must be counted to him as a defect, it is a defect which he shares with two of the master names of English literature—with Milton and with Wordsworth.   With Milton, indeed, Burke has many qualities in common.   We mark in both the same indomitable spirit which shrank from no labour and feared not the face of man, the same profound self-respect, the same magnanimous egotism (if one may use the phrase), even the same little asperities of temper, although to Burke's credit one must add that in the main he is free from the scurrility and coarseness which shock us in the prose writings of one so enamoured of ideal beauty as the author of *Comus* and *Paradise Lost*.

We must not then claim for Burke that he was a humorist.   Mr. Morley has also denied that he possessed true pathos.   One feels more difficulty in granting this, for one remembers—who, indeed, that reads it can forget ?—that immortal passage in the *Letter to a Noble Lord* in which Burke deplores the death of his son.   Grief never found a nobler expression than this ; in the rolling and solemn diction one seems to hear the 'large utterance of the early gods.'   Yet it must be admitted that we do not find in Burke that sweet, natural, and winning pathos which wells up so freely and spontaneously in Shakespeare.   His power is tragic rather than properly pathetic.   The exquisite scene in which Desdemona sings the willow-song one can scarcely read without a catch in the voice and a strange sensation in the throat. But when the end comes, and Othello dies by his own hand, who does not feel that tears were merely an impertinence?   We may apply this to Burke, and say that if such passages as that referred to are not properly to be described as pathetic, it is because in them Burke is on that higher plane where pathos is, as it were, swallowed up and transcended by tragedy.

Burke commenced author (to use an eighteenth-century phrase) with a brilliant and audacious parody of Bolingbroke.[1]   In the eyes of his contemporaries Bolingbroke filled a place for which we now find it somewhat hard to account.   Of that brilliant and nervous eloquence which secured him the title of the English Alcibiades no fragment now remains ; we can form our judgment of it only from his published writings.   Even the facts that he fills a niche in Thackeray's most perfect

---

[1] *A Vindication of Natural Society*, 1756.

novel, and that Mr. Churton Collins has given to the world a brilliant and highly finished study of his career, have scarcely sufficed to keep his fame alive. With many admirable talents he lacked solidity and character. At heart a sceptic, he was the idol of the High Church party and the strenuous promoter of severe repressive measures against the Dissenters. After his intrigues with the Pretender had shattered his party and shut him out from the *rôle* of an English statesman, he found consolation in playing at being a philosopher. He became the 'guide, philosopher, and friend' of Pope, and to him the credit—such as it is—of the plan and ideas of the *Essay on Man* belongs. His heterodox opinions in religion were concealed until the posthumous publication of his works under the superintendence of David Mallet. They came as a shock to most of his admirers, and Johnson may be assumed to have voiced the feelings of orthodoxy when, in his full-mouthed style, he denounced Bolingbroke as a scoundrel and a coward—a scoundrel for having held such views, and a coward for having dissembled them.

Burke's design, as he found it necessary to explain, was to show that the blunderbuss which, according to Johnson, Bolingbroke had aimed at religion, could be as effectively directed against the whole structure of civil society. To revealed religion Bolingbroke had opposed what it was then fashionable to call 'natural' religion. Burke in the same way contrasts artificial with natural society. The passages full of a sombre and dark-hued eloquence in which he paints the miseries of wars of conquest would win the approval of a member of the Peace Society; his description of the tyranny everywhere exercised over men, whether under the form of absolute monarchy, aristocracy, or democracy, would have called a smile of sardonic approval to the lips of the author of *Gulliver's Travels*. The 'law's delays' have been the frequent theme of the satirist, but never have they been better handled than by Burke. The fatiguing and degrading toil to which the great mass of human beings are every-where condemned is pictured with a vividness and a concentrated power which Karl Marx him-self might have envied. And all these evils sprang from the institution of artificial society, for what were wars and laws and forms of govern-ment but its creatures? The conclusion was obvious. If the errors and crimes of the advocate of revealed religion constituted a reason for ab-juring their faith, the same inexorable logic called upon men to destroy that artificial society which had brought such misery and ruin on their heads, and return to a state of nature. 'Show me,' cried Burke, 'any mischief produced by the madness or wickedness of theologians, and I will show you an hundred resulting from the ambition and villainy of conquerors and statesmen. Show me an absurdity in religion, and I will undertake to show you an hundred for one in political laws and institutions. . . . If, after all, you should confess these things, yet plead the necessity of political institutions, weak and wicked as they are, I can argue with equal, perhaps superior force, concerning the necessity of artificial religion ; and every step you advance in your argument you add a strength to mine. So that if we are resolved to submit our reason and our liberty to civil usurpation, we have nothing to do but to conform as quietly as we can to the vulgar notions which are connected with this, and take up the theology of the vulgar along with their politics.'

The fate of the *Vindication* was extremely curious. The book was justly regarded as an astonishing *tour de force*. But the subtlety and dexterity of its line of argument were not at first recognised, although the drift of the passage cited might seem obvious enough. Even scholars and men of the world like Chesterfield and Warburton were imposed upon ; they thought that the hand was really Bolingbroke's, and that the erratic statesman, after doing his worst on religion, had attempted a still more daring and deadly assault on civil society. When the author of a satire finds it necessary to explain that he was not serious, he must be assumed to have missed his mark. Irony, it would seem, is a dangerous weapon for a publicist to handle, as Defoe had experienced when he found in the pillory the answer to his *Short Way with the Dissenters.*[1] It is perhaps not altogether fanciful to see in the fate of Burke's maiden effort an illustration of his want of tact, of that tendency to go over the heads of his audience of which even nearly thirty years' experience of the House of Commons did not cure him. The publicist who is not merely studious of artistic form, but who wishes to produce a practical effect, must never allow himself to forget the 'average man'; Burke, on the other hand, constantly wrote and spoke as if the average man did not exist. If he was too subtle even for Chesterfield and Warburton, what could the crowd be expected to make of him?

For the reader who sits down to-day to the

[1] Another illustration from the case of a contemporary statesman may be pardoned. Probably nine out of every ten men think that Mr. Balfour's *Philosophic Doubt* is a sceptical work. They would be astonished if they were told that Mr. Balfour's 'philosophic doubts' concern, not the credibility of religion, but the 'oppositions of science.'

Vindication, perhaps its chief interest lies in the piquant contrast which it presents to the whole spirit and tenor of Burke's profoundest beliefs. To take only one example : let us put alongside of each other the lively and spirited remonstrance which he addresses to the 'high priests of the temple of justice,' and the noble eulogy of the law in his *Speech on American Taxation* (1774). 'I am innocent, gentlemen, of the darkness and uncertainty of your science. *I* never darkened it with confused notions, nor confounded it with chicane and sophistry. You have excluded me from any share in the conduct of my cause; the science was too deep for me ; I acknowledged it ; but it was too deep even for yourselves ; you have made the way so intricate that you are yourselves lost in it ; you err, and you punish *me* for your errors.' Now let us turn to the passage in which he declares that 'the law is in my opinion one of the first and noblest of human sciences, a science which does more to quicken and invigorate the human understanding than all the other kinds of learning put together.'

From another point of view, also, the *Vindication* is highly interesting to the student of Burke's intellectual processes. It proves his sensitiveness to the atmosphere of the time ; it shows that his quick and vigilant eye had thus early detected the

D

ultimate outcome of the loose rein now given to speculation on the bases of religion. He saw that men who would not quietly accept the faith of their fathers because it *was* the faith of their fathers would not be content to stop there; that they would soon proceed to call upon civil society also to produce its credentials and justify its existence to the logical reason. That his foresight was accurate is sufficiently proved by the fact that men like Rousseau and Godwin accepted as axioms what was to Burke a *reductio ad absurdum*. It would have been one of the strangest phenomena in the history of human thought had his book contributed to help forward the movement which he was to expend the last years of his life in combating with an almost unparalleled vehemence and pertinacity. How near it came to this one may guess from the fact that Godwin held that Burke had in the *Vindication* really proved what he intended to prove ironically. One certainly takes a very different impression from the *Vindication* than from the *Reflections on the French Revolution*. But the legitimate inference is, not that Burke was inconsistent, but that his preference for the old order of things sprang from no shallow or unthinking optimism. If he held that Society, constituted even as French society was before the Revolution, was a great blessing, he was not, therefore, blind to its defects and its evils. It was his profound belief that these were in the nature of things, that the good immeasurably outweighed the evil, that what was proposed in its place was but the ' airy fabric of a vision,' spun out of the delusive theories of the ' young men who see visions and the old men who dream dreams.'

In the same year as the *Vindication* (1756), appeared the well-known treatise on the *Sublime and Beautiful.* The book is one of that class of works ' without which no gentleman's library is complete '—books, that is, of which every one has heard, but into which few nowadays think of looking. The reasons for the comparative neglect into which a performance so vigorous and striking has fallen are not far to seek. Here, more than anywhere else in Burke, we feel the cold and sharp air of the eighteenth century—the critical century *par excellence*, the age of prose and reason. The book, with its air of scientific thoroughness, its close and careful analysis of those qualities and objects which rouse in us the sense of the sublime and the beautiful, fell in with the taste of the time ; but such speculations have now gone sadly out of fashion. We feel that it is out of place to carry into a thing so soft, fluid, and many-hued as literature the rigorous logic which

is appropriate and necessary in the severer
sciences. Like Addison's *Essay on the Imagination*, like his more celebrated criticism of *Paradise
Lost*, the whole performance strikes a modern
reader as rather arid and frigid. Burke often
awakens a sense of the sublime; never less so
than in the treatise which goes by that name.
Artistic and æsthetic criticism has, in this country
at least, gone on widely different lines from those
laid down by Burke; it has laid aside its severely
philosophic dress, and sought to charm rather
than to convince. And in its method it may be
said to have adopted the very system which
Burke explicitly condemns. 'One signal merit,'
says Mr. Morley, 'remains to the *Inquiry*. It
was a vigorous enlargement of the principle,
which Addison had not long before timidly illus-
trated, that critics of art seek its principles in the
wrong place so long as they limit their search to
poems, pictures, engravings, statues, and build-
ings, instead of first arranging the sentiments and
faculties in man to which art makes its appeal.'
The advocacy of this system may be a 'signal
merit,' but the method of modern criticism has
been quite the reverse; it has sought—and surely
not altogether unsuccessfully—to draw the rules
of art from a reverent study of the masters of
golden speech, the masterpieces of antique art.

In Germany, however, Burke's influence has been more apparent. His book, on its first appearance, had the good fortune to attract the attention of a mind at once so receptive and so original as that of Lessing, and that author, then meditating the *Laocoön*, a work which makes an epoch in criticism, set about translating and annotating Burke's *Inquiry*. It is also said to have interested and stimulated Kant. And, indeed, the *Inquiry* is admirably suited to the German mind, with its love of scientific precision and thoroughness, its passion for classification, for reducing everything to rule and system. We may conceive the delight with which a German logician would read the admirably reasoned passages in which Burke proves, with perhaps a superfluity of illustration, that beauty has no necessary connection with proportion or utility. He might at the same time quarrel with Burke's rather arbitrary use of certain terms, as when he speaks of delight as a neutral sort of feeling, whereas in common parlance delight is a livelier form of pleasure, or again when he calls awe and reverence subordinate degrees of astonishment.

But when all possible deductions are made, it must be granted that the *Inquiry* bears the impress of a powerful and vigorous mind. And it must be remembered that it was written at an age when most men, if their thoughts turn to literature at all, are writing love-poems or idle tales. It is characteristic of Burke's intellectual strenuousness, that even in what we may term his relaxations he exhibits the same grave sincerity, the same anxiety to penetrate beneath the superficial show of things to their inner and vital spirit, which were to mark his writings on subjects which the practical world considers as of more importance ; that he should throw himself into the discussion of the principles of art with something of the same ardour as he brought to the study of the means by which great empires are built up and held together. To the merely literary student Burke's treatise is interesting as showing his preferences in poetry. It is significant of his taste that most of his quotations should be drawn from Milton ; doubly significant when we remember that Pope and the polished school were then at the zenith of their fame. It would be wrong to rank the book among Burke's best efforts, but it is of high value as one of the many proofs of the catholicity of his intellectual interests. In the preface, he asks characteristically, 'What subject does not branch out to infinity? It is precisely in awakening this sense of spaciousness, in opening wide vistas of speculations before our eyes, that a great part of Burke's enduring power over our minds resides.

The two books which have been passed in review gave Burke a high place in the republic of letters. Horace Walpole tells us of his having met, in 1761, 'a young Mr. Burke, who wrote a book in the style of Lord Bolingbroke, which is much admired. He is a sensible man, but has not worn off his authorism yet, and thinks there is nothing so charming as writers, and to be one. He will know better one of these days.' To the last, Burke retained a keen interest in the *belles-lettres*, but he soon discovered that his true bent was towards politics. In 1765 he became private secretary to Lord Rockingham, and in the same year he entered Parliament. He had now come into his kingdom; he had found his true sphere. He brought to his task a full, indeed an over-flowing mind; as he proudly says of himself (*Letter to a Noble Lord*), he did not go into Parliament to con his lesson. His speeches on the Stamp Act at once drew the eyes of the town to him. They elicited a compliment from Pitt, still the Great Commoner, and Johnson wrote exultingly to Langton that Burke had gained more reputation than perhaps any man had gained by his first appearance before. Burke, however, was to labour for his party by his pen as well as by his oratory, and four years after his entry into Parliament he gave the world the first taste of his quality as a political pamphleteer. His *Observations on the Present State of the Nation* is usually passed by with scantier notice than the striking merit of the pamphlet seems to demand. It is, first of all, a magnificent piece of polemics, and the Whigs who followed the lead of Lord Rockingham must more than ever have congratulated themselves on the accession of Burke to their ranks. The pamphlet to which Burke's was a reply was the production of George Grenville, then considered the foremost authority among English statesmen on matters of finance and commerce.[1]   Burke was, however, more than a match for him on his own ground, and he overwhelms him both with facts and with grave and weighty irony. On several grounds the pamphlet is remarkable. It contains the germ of Burke's great speeches on the American question. In it he predicts thus early a convulsion in France from the deplorable condition of her finances, in opposition to Grenville, who had laboured to prove that they were in a much sounder condition than those of England. Here, too, we come for the first time upon a clear and definite statement

[1] Johnson's exquisite, but rather unjust, sarcasm on Grenville, is worth quoting: 'He had powers not universally possessed: could he have enforced payment of the Manilla ransom, *he could have counted it.*'

of that doctrine to which Burke held fast through the whole of his life—the doctrine that in politics expediency, conceived in no ignoble sense, is the highest wisdom, and that in this sphere abstract reasoning is likely only to dazzle and to mislead. 'Politics,' he maintains, 'ought to be adjusted, not to human reasonings, but to human nature ; of which reason is but a part, and by no means the greater part.'   'Men of sense, when new projects come before them, always think a discourse proving the mere right or the mere power of acting in the manner proposed to be no more than a very unpleasant way of misspending time.   They must see the object to be of proper magnitude to engage them ; they must see the means of compassing it to be next to certain ; the mischiefs not to counterbalance the profits ; they will examine how a proposed imposition or regulation agrees with the opinion of those who are likely to be affected by it; they will not despise the consideration even of their habitudes or prejudices. . . . They well know that an attempt towards a compulsory equality in all circumstances, and an exact defini-tion of the supreme rights in every case, is the most dangerous and chimerical of all enterprises. The old building stands well enough, though part Gothic, part Grecian, part Chinese, until an attempt is made to square it into uniformity.

Then it may come down upon our heads altogether in much uniformity of ruin; and great will be the fall thereof.' The passage just quoted bore special reference to the schemes for taxing America. When Burke severed himself from his party on the French Revolution, he was charged with apostasy from the principles which he had till then professed. To this charge it is surely sufficient to answer that the passage cited above, and which is only one of a hundred which might be brought forward, is in exact accordance with the principles on which he condemned the French Revolution. The circumstances have changed, but the principles remain the same, and whole passages might be transferred from the *Observations* of 1769 to the *Reflections* of 1790 without shocking any one with the slightest sense of incongruity. In truth, the charge of inconsistency is almost ludicrously inapplicable to Burke ; it may safely be asserted that the life of no public man was more uniform in texture, more of a piece, than that of the subject of this sketch. Strip him of this, as he proudly said, and you leave him naked indeed.[1]

The *Thoughts on the Present Discontents*, which followed in rapid succession (1770), has been ranked by some critics first among Burke's works

---

[1] *Appeal from the New to the Old Whigs.*

in point of style. It was a bold book, being in essence nothing less than an impeachment of the King ; and although respectful in tone, it is in reality far more deadly, because more measured and better reasoned, than the smart invective, the epigrammatic terseness and point, of Junius. It is directed against what Burke considered a dangerous and insidious attempt to divorce the Ministry from the House of Commons by a system of double cabinets, and to increase the power of the Crown, no longer by the open use of prerogative, but by the secret employment of a corrupt influence. It seems clear that Burke's description of the means adopted to carry out this plan was, to some extent at least, elaborated out of his inner consciousness. Mr. Morley describes it as a 'structure of artificial rhetoric,' and Mr. Lecky[1] thinks it probable that Burke considerably exaggerated the systematic and elaborate character of the plan that was adopted. In order, however, to appreciate the *Thoughts*, a short historical retrospect is necessary.

George III. had come to the throne determined to be something more than a mere ornamental figurehead. To this design the great obstacle was that system of homogeneous administrations which had been the natural result of

---

[1] *History of the Eighteenth Century*, vol. iii. ch. x.

the gradual transference of the seat of authority from the Crown to the House of Commons. That system was not of long standing, and indeed its growth may be described as the result of a happy series of accidents. Under the Tudors and the Stuarts the Ministers were not considered as mutually responsible for the acts of the whole body; each was looked upon as the personal servant of the sovereign, and responsible only for his own department. The Revolution of 1789 brought about a profound and far-reaching change. In foreign affairs, indeed, William exercised a dominant influence; but in home politics his foreign origin, the instability of his throne, his lack of knowledge of the conditions of English public life, his desire to conciliate those to whom he owed his crown, and his absorption in the mighty confederation against Louis XIV., of which he was the life and soul, all conspired to make him leave the chief direction of affairs in the hands of the able Ministers whom he gathered around him. It was not, however, till the reign of the first two Georges that parliamentary government, directed by a homogeneous Ministry, with a Prime Minister at its head, began to settle down into something like its present form. George I. and George II. were foreigners like William, but they had not his strength of character, and they were even more ignorant than he of the manners and customs of English life. By the very necessity of the case, by the instinct of self-preservation, they were restricted in their choice of Ministers to one political party. The whole Tory party lay under the suspicion of being tainted with Jacobitism; and so long as any danger existed from the Pretender, it was impossible to intrust them with any of the chief posts of state. On the death of Anne their chiefs had intrigued for the restoration of the Stuarts; and when the prompt and resolute action of the Whig lords had defeated their designs, Bolingbroke fled into exile, took service under the Pretender, and vainly tried to instil some of his own daring energy into the feeble and flaccid counsels of that unhappy prince. The inevitable result had been to alienate the Crown from its natural supporters, the Tory party, to throw the new monarch into the hands of the great Whig oligarchy, and thus to perpetuate and fix the character impressed on the constitution by the Revolution. And in Walpole the Whigs found a leader who was resolved to be, in a sense in which no previous minister had been, first Minister of the Crown, and who would brook no insubordination among the members of his administration. It was

Walpole's long ascendency which gave our parliamentary system its present form, and he is perhaps the first minister in whom a Premier of to-day would recognise his prototype. Against that ascendency Bolingbroke waged a bitter but unavailing warfare. He had been permitted to return to England, but his seat in the Lords was not restored, and he was shut out from the House which had so often resounded with his brilliant eloquence. He turned to the press, but his brilliant diatribes in the *Craftsman* availed little to shake the power of a minister who had the Crown, the Whig oligarchy, and the whole commercial interest of the country on his side, and even the insensate outcry against the Excise Bill— the one great measure which broke the torpor of an administration almost unexampled in our annals for poverty of legislative achievement— only inflicted a temporary check on the prestige of Walpole. It was at last borne in upon Bolingbroke that so long as the Whigs held together and remained in alliance with the Crown there was no hope for the party of which he was the most brilliant ornament. His mind, somewhat shallow and superficial indeed, but amazingly fertile in expedients, conceived a new scheme, and his *Patriot King*, a book published after his death, became the text-book of those whose fine-spun theories Burke runs full tilt against in his *Thoughts on the Present Discontents.*

The ideal which Bolingbroke set up was, indeed, a very pleasing one to contemplate; but briefly, it was that of an enlightened and virtuous monarch who, in choosing his Ministers, would look, not at all to political ties, but only to personal character and ability. The prospect was very fascinating to those who saw only the evils and vices of party government; under such a king, corruption, the mainspring of Walpole's power, as it was unjustly said,[1] would cease, and political life would become cleaner and more wholesome. But a deeper analysis showed that the ideal— 'such was their cant' are Burke's emphatic words in refuting this charge against Walpole— was radically unsound, and that if it could have been realised in practice, it would virtually have reversed the whole course of development since the Revolution. As soon as that great event made Parliament practically supreme in the state, political stability could only be attained by the conduct of public affairs being placed in the hands of a compact body of men, holding the same political principles, and agreed upon a common course of policy; and this again implied government by party. Parliament was now to

[1] *Appeal from the New to the Old Whigs.*

rule; in order that it might do so with any degree of dignity and efficiency, it must have adequate guidance and direction. And how could it obtain such guidance if the Cabinet was a scene of divided counsels and irreconcilable principles, while the sovereign, whose personal ascendency had formerly held administrations together, was deprived of the power and authority which had enabled him to fulfil that function?

Clear, however, as this now seems to us in the light of later experience, the trend of events was as yet but dimly discerned, and George III. was able to make a determined, and all but successful, effort to recover the power which the Crown had lost at the Revolution. The circumstances, indeed, were singularly propitious for his design. All danger from the Pretender had now ceased; after the '45, indeed, Jacobitism was dead as a fighting force, though it survived as a sentiment, and country squires still drank to the king over the water, but were perfectly content that he should remain there. A great wave of loyalty swept over the country at the accession of George, and when he declared that, born and educated in this country, he gloried in the name of Briton, he struck a responsive chord in the heart of a people in whose national character jealousy of foreigners is a leading feature. The Tories felt that the time had come to emerge from their long retirement, and they rallied round the throne of a monarch who was understood to be anxious to throw off the yoke of the Whigs. The first step was to get rid of Pitt; and the great Commoner, whose splendid services might have secured him against even the proverbial ingratitude of princes, was driven to resign in 1761. Newcastle, contemptible, indeed, in character and ability, but powerful as the head of the Whig confederacy, soon followed. The war was brought to a close by a peace which brought indeed great gains to England, but gains which many considered as not at all commensurate to the exertions of England, and to the splendid military achievements which had marked its course. The king fixed upon the Earl of Bute—a mere court favourite, with no experience whatever, as the minister who was to inaugurate the new scheme of things. For the end in view the choice was unfortunate. The one thing certainly known of the new minister was that he was a Scotsman,[1] and the mass of Englishmen at this time hated the Scots as heartily as Johnson pretended to do. Bute soon found his position untenable, and the king turned to George Grenville, who called himself a Whig, but who was imbued with autocratic principles.

[1] Apparently no disqualification nowadays!

Burke himself has drawn, as only he can draw, the portrait of this statesman.[1]   Upright, honest, and well-meaning, admirably versed in parliamentary procedure, and with a knowledge of trade and finance then considered unrivalled, he was yet narrow, formal, and pedantic, incapable of taking broad and general views, and deplorably destitute of political tact.   In the course of his ill-omened administration he succeeded in sowing the seeds of the American War, and in setting the whole country in a flame, by the arbitrary and illegal proceedings against Wilkes.   But while these measures secured the hearty approval of the king, Grenville's want of tact made him personally displeasing to George.   He lectured and dogmatised in the royal audience-chamber, as he lectured and dogmatised in the House of Commons, till George exclaimed in a fit of petulance that he would rather see the devil in his closet than George Grenville.   Grenville fell in 1765, and the king was forced to call upon Rockingham to form a Ministry.   Rockingham was the friend and munificent patron of Burke, and the section of the Whigs of which he was the nominal head included the most honest body of politicians then in public life.   Almost alone they had resisted the disintegrating influences by which the king

---

[1] *Speech on American Taxation* (1774).

had contrived to break all political ties.   The
accession to office of the Rockingham Whigs was
a sign that for the time the king's plan had broken
down.   The new Ministers set themselves to undo
much of the evil that had been done by Grenville ; they pacified America by the repeal of the
Stamp Act, and by a series of liberal measures
conciliated popular feeling at home.   But a
Ministry so distasteful to the king could not last
long ; Chatham, whose support might have given
it stability, held aloof, and in 1766 the Rockingham Whigs were dismissed and Pitt was recalled
to office.   Despite the obsequious deference which
he paid to the king, Pitt was no favourite with
George, in whose eyes the great Commoner was
merely a trumpet of sedition.   In one most
essential point, however, he was in hearty accord
with his royal master—he shared George's dislike
of the system of party government.   These views
were reflected in the character of the strangely
composite and heterogeneous Ministry which he
formed, and of which Burke has left us so inimitable a description.[1]   He made, says Burke, a piece
of joinery so crossly indented and whimsically
dovetailed, such a piece of diversified mosaic, such
a tesselated pavement without cement, that it was
indeed a very curious show, but utterly unsafe to

[1] *Speech on American Taxation.*

touch and unsure to stand upon. The personal ascendency of Pitt was the one thing that held the Ministry together; but Pitt had hardly grasped the reins of power before he was laid aside by a mysterious illness, which utterly incapacitated him from attending to public business. No sooner had he disappeared from the scene than his colleagues, under the guidance of the brilliant Townshend, plunged into a series of disastrous conflicts. Chatham had gone further even than Burke and Rockingham in his support of the Americans; unwarned by the experience of Grenville's abortive attempt, Townshend proceeded to impose new import duties on articles entering America. The old struggle against Wilkes was renewed in an acuter phase, and the House of Commons set itself to defy the country, by transferring the rights of the electors of Middlesex to itself.

Such was the state of matters at home and abroad when Burke published the *Thoughts on the Present Discontents*. The attempt to dispense with party government, the attempt to realise Bolingbroke's ideal, had had a fair trial, and what were the results? Burke's answer was emphatic and damning. The government, he said, was at once dreaded and contemned. The laws were despoiled of all their respected and salutary terrors; their inaction was a subject of ridicule and their exertion of abhorrence. Our dependencies had slackened in their affections. We knew neither how to yield nor how to enforce. Disconnection and confusion, in office, in parties, in families, in parliament, in the nation, prevailed beyond the disorders of any former time. Corruption was practised more openly, and on a far more lavish scale, than in the 'bad old days' of Walpole.

Had Burke limited himself in the *Thoughts* to a description of the inner working of the cabal, his work would long since have ceased to interest any but the historical student. But, to a greater degree than almost any other of his books, the pamphlet is thick - sown with those profound maxims of political wisdom with which it is his especial distinction to illumine his discussion of the most ephemeral topics. In the true spirit of a statesman he proclaims that 'the temper of the people amongst whom he presides ought to be the first study of a statesman.' 'In all disputes between them and their rulers the presumption is at least upon a par in favour of the people. If this presumption in favour of the subjects against the trustees of power be not the more probable, I am sure it is the more comfortable speculation ; because it is more easy to change an administration than to reform a people.'

What then was Burke's remedy for the disorders of which he made so keen an analysis? It was simply a reversion to the system of government by party. To justify this system was, therefore, one of the main objects of the pamphlet. He did so in no shallow, optimistic spirit. He was fully alive to all that the speculative philosopher could urge against the system ; he was well aware that, considered in the abstract, party government was bound to appear a most curious and not very fascinating phenomenon. He did not wonder, he said, that the behaviour of many parties should have made persons of tender and scrupulous virtue out of humour with all sorts of connection in politics. He admitted that people acquire in such confederacies a narrow, bigoted, and pre-scriptive spirit, and that they are apt to sink the general good in this circumscribed and partial interest. But he maintained that such evils, real and glaring as they were, and are, were accidental, and not necessarily involved in the idea of party connection. 'Where duty renders a critical situa-tion a necessary one, it is our business to keep free from the evils attendant on it, and not to fly from the situation itself. If a fortress is seated in an unwholesome air, an officer of the garrison is obliged to be attentive to his health, but he must not desert his station.' . . . 'When a public man omits to put himself in a situation of doing his duty with effect, it is an omission that frustrates the purposes of his trust almost as much as if he had formally betrayed it. It is surely no very rational account of a man's life that he has always acted right, but has taken special care to act in such a manner that his endeavours could not possibly be productive of any consequence.' . . . 'Party,' he continues, 'is a body of men united for promoting by their joint endeavours the national interest upon some particular principle in which they are all agreed. For my part, I find it impossible to conceive that any one believes in his own politics, or thinks them to be of any weight, who refuses to adopt the means of having them reduced into practice.' He proceeds to define the limits within which the subordination of one's own opinions to those of one's party is permissible, and even laudable. 'Men thinking freely will in particular instances think differently. But still, as the greater part of the measures which arise in the course of public business are related to or dependent on some great leading general principles in government, a man must be peculiarly unfortunate in the choice of his political company if he does not agree with them nine times out of ten.' . . . 'When the question is in its nature doubtful, or not very material, the modesty which becomes an individual, and (in spite of our court moralists) that partiality which becomes a well-chosen friendship, will frequently bring on an acquiescence in the general sentiment. Thus the disagreement will naturally be rare ; it will only be enough to indulge freedom, without violating concord or disturbing arrangement. And this is all that ever was required for a character of the greatest uniformity and steadiness in connection.' . . . 'Of what sort of material,' he asks, 'must that man be made, how must he be tempered and put together, who can sit whole years in Parliament with five hundred and fifty of his fellow-citizens, amidst the storm of such tempestuous passions, in the sharp conflict of so many wits and tempers and characters, in the agitation of such mighty questions, in the discussion of such vast and ponderous interests, without seeing any one sort of men whose characters, conduct, and disposition would lead him to associate himself with them, to aid and be aided in any one system of public utility?'

Burke's innate conservatism displayed itself when he came to consider the particular measures then advocated for the removal of the evils he describes. The skill with which he conducts his analysis of these evils is only equalled by the poverty of the reforms he proposes, a poverty in

which his book resembles nothing so much as
Carlyle's *Chartism* and *Past and Present.* The
one practical measure which he proposes is that
frequent and correct lists of voters in the princi-
pal divisions should be made out, in order that
the people might judge of the conduct of their
constituents.   Against the favourite proposals
for triennial parliaments and a place-bill he set
himself like a flint. Distrust and dislike of all
organic change, of all tampering with the Constitution, were with him a ruling passion. To his
vivid historic imagination the British Constitution,
as settled at the Revolution, was the last word of
political wisdom. To lay violent hands on any
part of it seemed to him almost an act of sacrilege.
'We ought,' he cried vehemently at a later day,
'to understand it according to our measure, and
to venerate where we are not able presently to
comprehend.'[1] Such language sounds strange to
modern ears ; and there can be little doubt that
Burke's admiration of the British parliamentary
system was tinged by something like superstition.
With the best will in the world one might surely
confess oneself unable to venerate the system of
rotten boroughs, although it is easy enough to
understand their *raison d'être.* But Burke clung
even to the rotten boroughs; and throughout his

---

[1] *Appeal from the New to the Old Whigs* (1791).

career he consistently opposed all attempts to lower the suffrage, or to give representatives to the manufacturing towns which were rapidly springing up.   If it is asked how it is possible to reconcile his conduct in this respect with his maxim of 'the presumption being on a par in favour of the people,' the solution would to Burke have seemed easy enough.   He drew a strong and sharp distinction between practical grievances and abstract rights.   He held that the people were admirable judges of practical oppressions;[1] but to understand the true cause, and to bring about the real cure, were both beyond their province.   The patient must judge whether he is well or ill; but to discover the disease, and apply appropriate remedies, is the part of the skilled physician.   If, indeed, the physician pockets his fee and neglects his patient, there is a call for inquiry, but we are not on that account to fall back on quackery and empiricism.

Burke's view of the relations which ought to exist between a member of Parliament and his constituents followed naturally from these principles.   In 1774 he stood for Bristol, and was returned.   During the stirring times which had followed the action of the House of Commons in the Wilkes affair, it had become the fashion for

[1] *Letter to Sir Hercules Langrishe* (1792).

the constituencies to send express instructions to
their representatives as to their conduct in the
House. Burke's colleague in the representation
of Bristol declared after the poll that he would
feel himself bound to obey such mandates. Even
in this moment of triumph, when a temporary
expansion might have been pardoned, Burke
was on the alert to assert his independence.
'Certainly, gentlemen,' he said,[1] 'it ought to be
the happiness and glory of a representative to
live in the strictest union, the closest correspondence, and the most unreserved communication with his constituents. Their wishes ought to
have great weight with him; their opinions high
respect, their business unremitted attention. It
is his duty to sacrifice his repose, his pleasure,
his satisfactions to theirs; and above all, ever,
and in all cases, to prefer their interest to his
own. But his unbiassed opinion, his mature
judgment, his enlightened conscience he ought
not to sacrifice to you, to any man, or to any set
of men living. *Your representative owes you not
his industry only, but his judgment; and he betrays
instead of serving you if he sacrifices it to your
opinion.*' When, six years afterwards, he was
fighting a losing battle in the same city against
the forces of bigotry and intolerance, his language

[1] *Speech after the Poll at Bristol* (1774).

was no less emphatic. ' I was to look indeed,' he declared, ' to your opinions, *but to such opinions as you and I must have five years hence. I was not to look to the flash of the day.* I knew that you chose me in my place along with others to be a pillar of the state, and not a weathercock on the top of the edifice, exalted for my levity and versatility, and of no use but to indicate the shiftings of every fashionable gale.'[1] Is it too much to expect that our modern politicians should show a little of this independent spirit? Perhaps so; for if even in Burke's day the assertion of the right of a representative to form his own opinions and act upon them might cost him his seat, it has certainly become infinitely harder now when every vote recorded in the division lobby is known, every debate published and spread broadcast, every speech read and discussed. In a democratic constitution, it is a matter of infinite difficulty and delicacy to balance and adjust the rights of members of Parliament and the claims of their constituents. Difficult and delicate the business is, but unless our representatives are to be degraded into mere automatic machines, some solution must be found. It is the radical vice of democracy that under it

---

[1] *Speech at the Guildhall, Bristol* (1780)—one of the manliest, most admirable, and most dignified of his efforts.

the maintenance of any high ideal of statesman-
ship becomes almost impossible. In Burke's
felicitous phrase, our statesmen are under a constant and all but irresistible temptation to look
only to the flash of the day. Our leaders, it is
the common complaint, no longer lead ; they do
not seek to form and mould public opinion ; in
the cant phrase of the day, they think it no
business of theirs to 'make planks,' but merely to
be floated down into office upon them. The
dictates of reason are hushed before the whisper
of the caucus and the report of the party whip.
We have great need of a Burke to protest alike
by his voice and by his example against a conception of the statesman's function so mean and
ignoble as this.

If Burke shrank with an exaggerated dread
from the mere hint of any organic change in the
Constitution, he was instrumental in bringing
about many practical reforms. His scheme of
Economical Reform will fall to be discussed
later on. He vigorously supported the repeal
of the cruel and foolish insolvency laws which
then defaced the statute-book, and in his Bristol
speech of 1780 he took occasion to pay a magnificent tribute to the philanthropic labours of
Howard. Capital punishment was in the eighteenth
century inflicted for offences comparatively

trifling, and the number of executions seems to modern ideas enormous. Burke strove hard to mitigate the ferocity of the law in this respect. After the Gordon riots (1780) he pressed on the authorities, with characteristic eagerness and with characteristic keenness of logic, the cruelty and futility of executing a large number of the rioters. His efforts were all the nobler because he had not the slightest sympathy with the objects or passions of the rioters; indeed, it was his support of the Catholic relief measures which alienated many of his supporters at Bristol. The subject of slavery engaged his earnest attention, and among his works is to be found the sketch of a Negro Code. He feared that the entire abolition of slavery was impracticable, but he hoped that it might be so regulated as to produce the minimum of misery and oppression. Adam Smith is said to have told Burke that he was the only man who, without previous communication, thought on matters of trade and commerce exactly as he did. It does not appear, however, from Burke's published writings that he was a consistent or thoroughgoing advocate of the principle of free trade, although his *Thoughts and Details on Scarcity*, and detached passages in others of his writings, show that, on some points at least, he was in hearty accord with the author of the

Wealth of Nations. He took a leading part in advocating the measure which secured the freedom of the press by transferring the decision as to whether a publication was or was not libellous from the judge to the jury.

On the great question of religious toleration, also, Burke showed himself more liberal than most of his contemporaries, though less so than some. For the Roman Catholic Church—that mighty mother of the churches with her historical associations, her high and haughty claims, her imposing rites and ceremonies, her majestic unity —he had a warm and kindly feeling; for that spurious Protestantism which finds in hatred of the Pope an easy and convenient substitute for the love of God, he had nothing but contempt. He strenuously supported the repeal of the odious and oppressive statutes which put Roman Catholics at the mercy of the meanest informer; and even the outburst of religious fanaticism which culminated in the Gordon riots did not make him flinch in his policy. On the other hand, he opposed the petition of the Established clergy to be released from subscription to the Thirty-nine Articles, holding, with show of reason, that it was absurd for the state to lend the weight of its authority to an undefined system of church dogma. In his attitude towards the Dissenters he was not quite consistent, for although he at first supported their claim to be exempted from subscribing the Articles, when the Unitarians came forward to claim toleration he opposed their cause. He justified his opposition by alleging that the Unitarians were a political as well as a religious sect, that they were in sympathy with the French Revolution, and consequently enemies of the Constitution; and he drew a distinction between old and long-established sects whose principles and conduct were known, and new bodies which might, for all one knew, be hotbeds of anarchy and revolution.

It is time now to turn to Burke's speeches and writings on the American question. The war which was brought to a close by the Peace of Paris (1763) is one of the most glorious in our annals. But military glory is commonly bought for a price, and Pitt's triumphs had left England burdened with an enormous addition to her National Debt. The American Colonies had been perhaps the chief gainers by the war; for the expulsion of the French from Canada and the Spanish from Florida had removed the gravest danger which menaced the future of the English colonists. By the conquest of Canada the greatest obstacle to the expansion of the English-speaking race in

America had been swept away. In these circumstances, it was not at all unnatural that English statesmen should have thought it only right that America should contribute something more than she had hitherto done towards the defence of the Empire to which they looked for protection, and which had just put forth such mighty efforts on their behalf. It is important that this should be emphatically stated, for historians have shown themselves too much disposed to adopt without adequate inquiry the sentiments and the language of 4th of July orators, and they have for the most part made little effort to enter into the feelings of the statesmen who were responsible for the measures which brought on the rupture.

Till the accession of Grenville to office in 1765 the colonists had been left pretty much to themselves ; by a wise and salutary neglect, a generous nature, as Burke finely said, had been suffered to take her own way to perfection. It has been said, with almost as much truth as wit, that Grenville lost the Colonies because he read the American despatches, which none of his predecessors ever did. The Commercial Code, indeed, seems to modern ideas sufficiently severe and restrictive. The trade of America was made wholly subservient to that of the mother-country by a highly complex code of regulations and

restrictions. But the *Wealth of Nations* had not
yet appeared ; the Navigation Laws were still
the object of an unthinking idolatry ; and the commercial policy of England towards her Colonies,
however ungenerous and unwise it now seems,
was, as Adam Smith himself showed, incompar-
ably more liberal than that pursued by any other
European nation. The colonists as yet hardly
felt the restrictions imposed on their trade as
sensible grievances. The laws which amounted
to a practical prohibition of all manufactures in
America were little resented, for America had not
yet reached the manufacturing stage. Her most
valuable and characteristic products found a ready
market in Britain, and the home-country bound
itself to buy certain articles from the Colonies
alone. The most oppressive duties were evaded
by an immense and organised system of smuggling, carried on with the greatest boldness and
openness, and almost with the tacit connivance
of the home authorities. An extreme case is
mentioned by Mr. Lecky. During the French
War, a war in which the very existence of the
Colonies was at stake, it was found that the
Americans were supplying the French with stores
and provisions, and to England's indignant remonstrance it was coolly and cynically rejoined
that it was good policy to make as much as

possible out of the enemy! To a man of Grenville's temperament—at once that of an autocrat and of a precisian—all this could not but be profoundly abhorrent. To one who prided himself on his skill in finance, and who took so gloomy a view of the internal resources of England,[1] it was a supreme object to reduce the National Debt. He would have echoed the description of England given by a poet of our own day, as

> 'Bearing on shoulders immense,
> Atlantëan, the load,
> Well-nigh not to be borne,
> Of the too vast orb of her fate.'

Under the influence of these ideas he set to work with a characteristic energy and a characteristic want of tact. He took vigorous measures to enforce the Navigation Laws and to repress smuggling. Had he been content to stop there, his proceedings would undoubtedly have caused some outcry and irritation in the Colonies, but no one would have thought of denying the perfect legality and competence of his measures. It had been recognised over and over again that England possessed the right of legislating for the regulation of the commerce of the whole empire.

---

[1] See *The Present State of the Nation* and Burke's *Observations* thereon.

But Grenville's views went far beyond this. He resolved to establish permanently a portion of the British army in the Colonies, and to pay its cost by the proceeds of a stamp-duty on legal documents issued in America. For this purpose the famous Stamp Act was introduced in 1765. It attracted less attention than is given to an Indian Budget to-day. Burke was present in the gallery, and he tells us that he had rarely heard a more languid debate. No one seems to have had the slightest suspicion of the pregnant nature of the measure. As soon as the news was carried across the Atlantic, the Colonies were in a flame. Parliament, it was said, was assuming a new and unheard-of claim. It was practically proposing to tax them without their consent. If the claim were submitted to, their whole property was at the mercy of the home-country. To resist that claim was as much their duty as it was the duty of Hampden to resist the arbitrary impositions of Charles I. That taxation and representation went together was one of the fundamental maxims of the British Constitution, and its validity was not destroyed by the practical difficulties in the way of an American representation in Parliament.[1]

[1] These difficulties were humorously exhibited by Burke in *Observations on the Present State of the Nation.*

They drew a distinction which was to play a great part in the controversy between legislation designed primarily for the regulation of commerce and taxation for the purposes of revenue. The former they admitted to be the indisputable and prescriptive right of the British Parliament; the latter had hitherto been strictly reserved to their own legislative assemblies. This distinction, it is true, seems now rather vague and shadowy, and the English advocates of Grenville's measures were soon to prove with an unhappy and perverted ingenuity—what no one would now think of denying—that the Navigation Laws in reality imposed a most onerous and oppressive tax on American industry. The object for which the taxation was imposed was quite as distasteful to the colonists as the scheme itself. They shared the English distrust of standing armies, and it was feared that the British forces stationed in America, ostensibly for the purpose of protecting it from invasion by the French and the destructive raids of the savage Indians, were in reality intended to strengthen the hands of the executive power in the States, and perhaps for the ultimate destruction of the democratic form of liberty which they enjoyed in common.

The extreme gravity of the situation soon became apparent. Riots broke out in the States.

All the stamps on which the colonists could lay hands were destroyed. The newly appointed collectors were intimidated from exercising their functions. It became clear that if a struggle was to be averted the Act must be rescinded. The way was paved for its repeal when Grenville fell and Lord Rockingham came into office. The new Ministry adopted a twofold line of policy. They repealed the Stamp Act; but they accompanied the repeal by a Declaratory Act asserting the supreme right of Parliament to legislate for the Colonies in all circumstances whatsoever. In Burke's balanced sentences, 'they preserved the authority of Great Britain; they preserved the equity of Great Britain; they made the Declaratory Act; they repealed the Stamp Act. They did both fully, because the Declaratory Act was without qualification, and the repeal of the Stamp Act total.'

The effect of this eminently wise and healing measure was immediate. The storm subsided as rapidly as it had arisen. The Americans were gratified by the total repeal of the obnoxious Act, and they paid little attention to the mere idle recital of a right which it was assumed Great Britain never intended to exercise. The prospect looked brighter still when Chatham succeeded Rockingham, for that great rhetorician had ranged himself still more decidedly on the side of the Colonies. He had gloried in those acts which Grenville's supporters denounced as rebellion. He had vehemently opposed the Declaratory Act, and had drawn an altogether untenable distinction between the right of legislation and that of taxation. But his practical withdrawal from all share in the conduct of affairs altered the whole complexion of things. The Duke of Grafton became the head of the curiously incoherent administration which Chatham had formed, but the real direction of its policy rested with the king himself, and George had never concealed his dislike to the repeal of the Stamp Act. In 1767 import duties were laid on certain articles entering America. The old scenes were renewed across the Atlantic. The administration partly gave way, and in 1769 all the duties were taken off save that on tea. It was admitted that only a trifling revenue could be expected from this source, especially as the Americans had entered into agreements to use no articles coming from England until the obnoxious duty was removed. But the English Ministers were resolute to maintain the duty in order to vindicate the authority of Parliament. The situation was now perilous in the extreme. War might break out at any moment. But a war with their kinsmen did not seem distasteful to the English Ministry, nor, one must add, to the English people. Never, indeed, had England entered on a contest with a lighter heart. The Americans were accused of cowardice; a regiment or two, it was thought, would be sufficient to bring them to their senses. The tea-riots at Boston in 1773 were followed by severe measures against the offending city. Its port was closed and its charter was annulled. In the interval between this time and the outbreak of hostilities Burke's two great speeches were delivered. A month after the second the two countries were at war.

There are no more pregnant lessons in the science of how to look at things so as to see them and into them, of how to distinguish between what is perennial from what is deciduous in a political question, than Burke's two speeches on *Taxation of the American Colonies* and on *Conciliation with America.* This is the opinion of Mr. James Russell Lowell,[1] a patriotic son of that country whose cause Burke was advocating in the speeches thus eulogised, but the praise is hardly too strong. Burke's genius never shone out in a clearer or more attractive light than in his utterances on this great question. One might extract from them a manual of political maxims.

---

[1] *Political Essays: The Independent in Politics.*

Here, for example, is a cluster of the golden
sayings which Burke lavishes with a prodigal
hand :—'It is impossible to answer for bodies of
men. But I am sure that the natural effect of
fidelity, clemency, and kindness in governors is
peace, good-will, order, and esteem on the part
of the governed.' . . . 'Nobody will persuade me,
when a whole people are concerned, that acts of
lenity are not means of conciliation.' . . . 'Great
and acknowledged force is not impaired either
in effect or in opinion by an unwillingness to
exert itself. The superior power may offer peace
with honour and with safety. Such an offer from
such a power will be attributed to magnanimity ;
but the concessions of the weak are the concessions of fear.' . . . Abstract rights are, in their
exercise under certain circumstances, 'the most
odious of all wrongs and the most vexatious of
all injustice.' . . . 'The question with me is not
whether you have a right to render your people
miserable, but whether it is not your interest to
make them happy. It is not what a lawyer tells
me I may do, but what humanity, reason, and
justice tell me I ought to do. Is a politic act
the worse for being a generous one ? Is no con-
cession proper but that which is made from your
want of right to keep what you grant ? Or does
it increase the grace or dignity of an odious

claim, because you have your evidence-room full of titles and your magazines stuffed with arms to enforce them? Of what avail are those titles and those arms when the reason of the thing tells me that the assertion of my title is the loss of my suit, and that I could do nothing but wound myself by the use of my own weapons?' . . . 'Providence has decreed vexation to violence and poverty to rapine.' . . . 'It is a great mistake to suppose that mankind follow up practically any speculative principle either of government or of freedom, as far as it will go in argument and logical illation. All government, indeed every human benefit, is founded on compromise and barter. We balance inconveniences; we give and take; we remit some rights that we may enjoy others; and we choose to be happy citizens, rather than subtle disputants. . . . Man acts from adequate motives relative to his interests, and not on metaphysical speculations.' . . . 'Magnanimity in politics is not seldom the truest wisdom; and a great empire and little minds go ill together.'

Burke's attitude towards the attempt to tax America was determined by his constant principle of expediency. The question of abstract right he set aside with the same disdain with which he was afterwards to treat the *Contrat Social* and the 'rights of man.' To his mind such arguments were mere babble—mischievous babble, too. Grant, in effect he said, that you possess the right to tax America, grant also that you have the power to enforce that right, which seems doubtful, in case the Americans should take arms to resist it : is it wise to make the attempt, things being as they are? ' I am not here going into distinctions of rights, not attempting to mark their boundaries. I do not enter into these metaphysical distinctions. I hate the very sound of them.' The distinction between external and internal taxation may be, as gentlemen of the Ministry assert, altogether untenable: the essential thing is that the Americans believe in the distinction, and are prepared to act upon it. Their logic may be weak, but their hearts are stout; you cannot falsify the pedigree of that fierce people: indeed, if you consider it, an Englishman is the unfittest person on earth to argue another Englishman into slavery. ' Be content,' he concludes, 'to bind America by laws of trade ; you have always done it. Let this be your reason for binding their trade. Do not burthen them with taxes: you were not used to do so from the beginning. Let this be your reason for not taxing. These are the arguments of states and kingdoms. Leave the rest to the schools ; for there only they may be discussed with safety.'

In none of his great speeches can one study Burke's oratorical methods to better advantage than in these on American taxation. Even his digressions are magnificent. His portraits of Chatham, Townshend, and Grenville are altogether admirable ; it is almost incredible that the author of these finely-touched and discriminating sketches should have been thought capable of perpetrating the vulgar and flaring caricatures of Junius. In the speech of 1775 he describes with an amazing felicity and fertility of illustration the national character of America, the growth of its population, its commerce, its agriculture, its fisheries, the form of its government, the religion of the people,[1] their education, and their temperament. This glowing picture seemed to the Ministerialists to prove only that America was a noble object, and worth fighting for. 'Certainly it is,' answered Burke, 'if fighting a people be the best way of gaining them. . . . A further objection to force is that you impair the object by your very endeavour to preserve it. The thing you

---

[1] 'The people are Protestants. . . . All Protestantism, even the most cold and passive, is a kind of dissent. But the religion most prevalent in our northern colonies is a refinement on the principle of resistance ; it is the *dissidence of dissent and the Protestantism of the Protestant religion.*' It is interesting to see the genesis of the phrase which in Arnold's hands became a weapon of offence against the Dissenters.

fought for is not the thing you recover, but
depreciated, sunk, wasted, and consumed in the
contest. *Nothing less will content me than whole
America.'*

These magnificent appeals fell on dead ears;
the whole country, indeed, soon caught the infection, and Burke could only look sadly on as war
grew daily more imminent. With the skirmish at
Lexington the last hope of peace died, and with
it the dream of a free and united Empire, em-
bracing all men of English blood and English
speech.   The providence of God so willed it,
says Hawthorne:[1] 'if England had been wise
enough to twine our new vigour round about her
ancient strength, her power would have been too
firmly established ever to yield, in its due season,
to the otherwise immutable law of imperial
vicissitude. The world might then have beheld
the intolerable spectacle of a sovereignty and
institutions, imperfect, but indestructible.' Out
of this those who please may draw what comfort
and consolation they may. But to most it will
perhaps appear that the old dream was a generous
and noble one, and that the progress of the world
did *not* demand that the British Empire should,
by the folly and rashness of its guardians, be
shattered and rent asunder, and to such Burke's

[1] *Our Old Home*, chap. i.

efforts to avert the catastrophe will seem noble and splendid, although, alas! unavailing.

While England was fast losing her hold over the American Colonies, a new empire was in the strangest fashion preparing for her in the remote East. The story of the growth of the British power in India reads like a fairy tale ; but alas! it is a fairy tale with dark and sinister elements. Macaulay has drawn a vivid picture of the state of disorganisation and anarchy into which India fell after the death of Aurungzebe, and he has described the astonishment with which the student of Indian history follows the rapid growth of the power of the East India Company. 'Scarcely any man,' says he, 'however sagacious, would have thought it possible that a trading company, separated from India by fifteen thousand miles of sea, and possessing in India only a few acres for purposes of commerce, would in less than a hundred years spread its empire from Cape Comorin to the eternal snow of the Himalayas ; would compel Mahratta and Mohammedan to forget their mutual feuds in common subjection ; would tame down even those wild races which had resisted the most powerful of the Moguls ; and having united under its laws a hundred millions of subjects, would carry its victorious arms far to the east of the Burrampooter and far to the west of the Hydaspes, dictate terms of peace at the gates of Ava, and seat its vassal on the throne of Candahar.'

It is impossible in an essay like this to detail the successive steps by which the immense empire passed into the hands of our countrymen. It must suffice to mention that about the middle of last century a short but decisive struggle took place between the French and the forces of the British East India Company ; that, by the daring and the splendid military talents of Clive, the contest ended in favour of the British, and that with Clive's victories the process began by which province after province passed into the hands of the Company. Unfortunately for the honour of Britain, the wisdom and moderation of their government of the country which had thus fallen into their hands was by no means commensurate with the splendour of their military successes. By a strange destiny a company of traders had become the masters of a mighty empire, and it could hardly be wondered at that they did not immediately rise to an adequate conception of their new character, or that they should have ruled India with the one object of extracting as much money out of it as possible. The unhappy natives were the victims of an extortion un-precedented even in India ; they saw their ancient chiefs set up and knocked down at the mere pleasure of their new masters, like so many ninepins ; their immemorial customs trampled upon by men who made no effort to enter into thoughts and feelings so different from those familiar to themselves. And against this tyranny they had no refuge ; dire experience had convinced them that they were no match for the British in the field.

Parliament could not long remain indifferent to the scenes which were being enacted in India. As early as 1772, a Committee had sat on Indian affairs ; Clive had been examined ‘like a sheep-stealer,’ as he bitterly complained, and neither his splendid services, nor the gallant attempt he had made during his last administration to check the abuses rampant in India, availed to save him from a vote of censure. The fact that the Company, despite the immense revenues which had passed into its hands, was in desperate financial straits made the intervention of the Government an absolute necessity. The truth was that the victories of Clive had completely changed the character of the Company, and with it the genius of its administration. The possession of the Company’s stock was no longer valued for the paltry dividend it might bring, but for the share it conferred in the patronage of India, in the appointment, that is, of the plunderers of that unhappy country. The servants of the Company had virtually become its masters; and while the Company was on the verge of bankruptcy, the writers who had gone out to India in a penniless condition were returning home with immense fortunes. The radical vices of this system of government cannot be better described than in the calm and measured words of Adam Smith. 'The real interests of the Company,' he writes, 'if they were capable of understanding it, is the same with that of the country; and it is from ignorance chiefly, and the meanness of mercantile prejudice, that they ever oppress it. But the real interest of the servants is by no means the same with that of the country, and the most perfect information would not necessarily put an end to their oppressions. The regulations, accordingly, which have been sent out from Europe, though they have been frequently weak, have upon most occasions been well-meaning. More intelligence, and perhaps less good meaning, has sometimes appeared in those established by the servants in India. *It is a very singular government in which every member of the administration wishes to get out of the country, and consequently to have done with the government, as soon as he can, and to whose interest, the day after he has left it, and carried his whole fortune with him, it is perfectly indifferent, though the whole country was swallowed up by an earthquake'* (*Wealth of Nations*, Book IV. chap. vii.). And again : 'No other sovereigns ever were, or from the nature of things could be, so perfectly indifferent about the happiness or misery of their subjects, the improvement or waste of their dominions, the glory or disgrace of their administration, as, from irresistible moral causes, the greater part of the proprietors of such a mercantile company are and must necessarily be.'

The first step in the transfer of the supreme power in India from the Company to the Crown was taken when Lord North's Government in 1773 assumed the power of nominating a Governor-General of Bengal who was also to exercise authority over the other presidencies. In view of later developments, it is curious to find that Burke vehemently opposed this measure, holding that it was an unwarrantable breach of the Company's charter. His opposition was, however, of no avail, and the new Governor-General and his Council set out for India. With Warren Hastings' departure for India as the first British Governor-General, Burke's more intimate connection with Indian affairs begins, and the names of these two great men are as inseparably linked together as those of Cicero and Verres.

The care which Burke had bestowed upon the affairs of India, and the strong impression which they had made upon his mind, were first made evident to the world by his great speech on the introduction of Fox's East India Bill (1784). Although the bill was introduced by Fox, it seems clear that it was really drafted by Burke.[1] In the eleven eventful years which elapsed between 1773 and 1784, Burke's mind had undergone a change. He was now convinced that it was impossible to leave the government of India in the hands of the Company. The bill accordingly proposed to supersede the Company by a Board of seven Commissioners, in whose hands the entire political powers over the provinces occupied by the British were to be placed. The Commissioners were to be nominated in the first instance by Parliament, and afterwards by the Crown. Their tenure of office was to be for five years, and they were removable on address from either House of Parliament.

The speech in which Burke supported the bill is one of the noblest specimens of his oratory. To the charge that it was an attack on the

---

[1] See the evidence on the point in Sir George Cornwall Lewis's *Administrations of Great Britain.*

chartered rights of men, Burke replied that the charter of the Company was a charter of monopoly. 'Magna Charta is a charter to restrain power and to destroy monopoly. The East India Charter is a charter to establish monopoly and to create power.' He argued that the powers conferred on the Company emanated from Parliament, and that if it were proved that these powers had been grossly and persistently abused, Parliament was not only justified in intervening, but was bound to do so. 'We sold, I admit, all that we had to sell; that is our authority, not our control. We had not a right to make a market of our duties.' It was very characteristic of Burke that he should have refused to discuss on general grounds the policy of leaving extensive political powers over a vast empire in the hands of a commercial company, his attitude in this respect being in contrast to that of Adam Smith. He could not agree with those who held that such a policy must inevitably be fatal to good government. 'With my particular ideas and sentiments, I cannot go that way to work. I feel an insuperable reluctance in giving my hand to destroy any established institution upon a theory, however plausible it may be. My experience in life teaches me nothing clear upon the subject. I have known merchants with the

sentiments and abilities of great statesmen ; and
I have seen persons in the rank of statesmen
with the conceptions and characters of pedlars.'
In words of scathing eloquence he laid bare the
abuses of the administration of Warren Hastings,
and drew a lurid picture of the state to which
India had been reduced under British rule.

The bill, however, touched too many interests
to be successful.   The objections to it, indeed,
were grave enough, and they were elaborated and
exaggerated by the skilful oratory of the younger
Pitt, who was just then rising into fame, and
already cherishing ambitious dreams.   The main
objection to which one can now allow weight
was that the new Commissioners must inevitably
be destitute of any acquaintance with Indian
administration.   But the defeat of the bill was
due to other influences.   Every corporation
trembled at the attack made upon the greatest
chartered company of the realm.   The Tories
represented the measure as a mere scheme to
transfer the patronage of India to a body of
Whig politicians.   The direct and indirect influence of the Company itself was immense, and
it was of course thrown into the scale against
the bill.   Constitutional pedants pointed out that
it was a novel and dangerous precedent for
Parliament to name the members of an executive

body. But the great objection to the bill of the Coalition was simply that it *was* the bill of the Coalition. Politics, like misfortunes, make us acquainted with strange bedfellows ; but there is hardly anything in the political history of our country so astonishing and inexplicable as the junction of Fox and Burke with the man whom they had denounced during the whole course of the American War with almost unexampled virulence. It offended and alienated the mass of the public, never in love with coalitions, and any measure proceeding from so unpopular a Government was certain to be closely and jealously scrutinised. The King, for once, was on the side of the people ; he had always hated Fox, and he now regarded North as a deserter. He took the extremely bold step of writing to Lord Temple that he would consider as a personal enemy any peer who voted for the bill. His tactics were entirely successful ; the bill was thrown out in the Lords, the Coalition Ministry was dismissed, and Pitt assumed the reins of power, which he was to hold through so many eventful years.

The rejection of the bill did not cause Burke to relax his efforts on behalf of the Indian subjects of the Crown. The following year witnessed the return to England of Warren Hastings, the man of all others whom Burke regarded as the incarnation of the vicious and tyrannical system of administration which prevailed in India. Burke at once gave notice that he would call attention to the conduct of Hastings. What followed is well known to every one ; for every one has read Macaulay's essay on Hastings—one of the most brilliant efforts of that great master of panoramic history.

That Burke was in some respects unjust to Hastings, that he did not make sufficient allowance for the exceptional difficulties of his position, is now generally admitted. If no man is a hero to his *valet de chambre*, every man, it would seem, is a hero to his biographer. The task of whitewashing stained reputations is a favourite one with the writers of our day; Mr. Froude has done his best for Henry VIII., Lord Wolseley has just published a vindication of Marlborough, and even Judas Iscariot does not lack his apologists and defenders. It would have been hard if Hastings had been left under the stigma placed on his name by the superb eloquence of Burke and the brilliant essay of Macaulay. For in truth there was much to be said in favour of Hastings to which Burke was in no mood to listen. He had shown himself one of the most capable administrators who had ever been intrusted with the immense task of shaping an empire out of anarchy and chaos. He had preserved the British power in India from the gravest perils. Of all this he might justly have exclaimed with Coriolanus, 'Alone I did it,' for his colleagues at the council-board sullenly opposed his every act, and the Directors at home gave him no support. The publications of Sir James Stephen and others seem to prove that the specific charges which Burke brought against Hastings—the execution of Nuncomer, the Rohilla War, the extortions practised on Cheyte Sing and on the Begums of Oude—were greatly over-coloured.

Of the eloquence with which Burke denounced the administration of Hastings it is difficult to speak in adequate terms. One's mind almost reels before the evidences of the immense and unwearied industry with which Burke had studied the history of India, its customs, and the peculiar temperament of its peoples, which these great orations display. Some of Burke's other speeches and writings are undoubtedly of more permanent interest and importance, but in none do we get a better notion of the full range and compass of his powers. There is hardly an oratorical device of which he does not show himself a complete master in these famous and memorable orations on the impeachment of Warren Hastings. The grave and impressive dignity with which he reminded the Lords of the importance of the duties imposed upon them, the vividness with which he conjured up a mental picture of the great empire which had been the theatre of the misdeeds of Warren Hastings, his keen, unsparing analysis of the genius and character of the East India Company, are all admirable in their way. And as the great orator warmed to his work and thundered against the crimes of Hastings, pouring forth invectives, pathos, irony, vituperation almost in a breath, even the most devoted admirers of the great pro-consul felt that his cause was lost. Perhaps the most impressive tribute ever paid to an orator was the confession of Hastings that during Burke's speech he felt like a criminal, conscious of his innocence as he was.

Mr. Morley, in one of the acutest and most admirable passages of an admirable book, has discussed the nature of Burke's sensibility to the wrongs and misdeeds which marked the British rule in India. He dismisses the idea that it sprang wholly or even mainly from a misty and vague philanthropy. 'It was,' says he, 'reverence rather than sensibility, a noble and philosophic conservatism rather than philanthropy, which raised the storm in Burke's breast against the rapacity of English adventurers in India and the imperial crimes of Hastings.' The importance of this fine and just criticism is that it enables us to see how Burke's attitude in regard to the affairs of India is related to his attitude in regard to the other great problems which came before him, in particular the French Revolution.

The impeachment dragged on for several years, and in the end Hastings was acquitted. The acquittal came to Burke as a blow, and even now one might be inclined to regard his intervention in Indian affairs as merely one of his splendid failures. But he had really done his work. He had awakened the national conscience. If since his time the whole spirit of Indian administration has changed, if India now enjoys under British rule a degree of peace and prosperity to which she had long been a stranger, no small share of the credit is due to the unwearied efforts of Burke, to the unselfish devotion which he gave to the cause of a people with whom he had no personal ties, and from whom he could expect no gratitude.

Burke's speech on *Economical Reform* only falls below the greatest of his efforts. He often tired his audience by his diffuseness and prolixity; he often shocked its not over-fastidious sense by his almost frenzied violence, his grievous sins against good taste. The speech under consideration is free from both defects; in taste and temper it is excellent. Gibbon, in his rather magniloquent way, testifies to the delight with which 'that ingenious and diffusive orator Mr. Burke' was listened to even by those whose existence he proscribed. The nature of the subject-matter did not lend itself to flights of gorgeous rhetoric; what makes the distinction of the speech is its temperate and statesmanlike tone, its clear and lucid handling of a complicated mass of detail, its strokes of humour and irony. Burke does not often seek to raise a laugh, and his success is not uniform when he does make the attempt. But it would surely be wrong to deny the merit of humour to the passage in the speech in which he describes the various titles and jurisdictions of the King, or to that other in which he recounts the 'famous history of the revenue adventures of the bold baron North and the good knight Probert upon the mountains of Venodotia.' And what could be keener than his sarcasm on the Board of Trade and Plantations? 'They understood decorum better; they knew that matters of trade and plantations are no business of theirs.'

To discuss Burke's speech on its literary merits alone would, however, be absurd. One of the difficulties in the way of an adequate appreciation of Burke is that in a special sense he belongs both to literature and to history.[1] The scheme

---

[1] It is a significant fact that Burke is the one English statesman of the first rank who has been accorded a place in the *English Men of Letters* series.

which Burke set forth in this famous speech was one of which the name ' Economical Reform ' gives an inadequate notion. The key to the spirit in which Burke approached the question is supplied by the first title of the bill : it was ' a plan for the better security of the independence of Parliament.' As we saw in discussing the *Present Discontents*, jealousy of the Crown, a dread that through the skilful use of its power of corrupt influence, the independence and authority of Parliament were steadily being sapped, while outwardly everything appeared as of old, were uppermost in the minds of the Rockingham Whigs. Burke avowed this plainly in the opening sentences of his speech.   These feelings had been strengthened by the disasters of the American War, a heavy share of the responsibility for which was placed on the shoulders of the King, while the onerous burdens which the struggle entailed could not but give weight to the purely economical reasons for reducing the expenses of administration so far as this could be done without impairing the efficiency of its working, or interfering unduly with established and prescriptive rights.

The scheme itself was admirably adapted for the end in view. It swept away a host of offices maintained for no public utility, but merely for the purposes of parliamentary corruption ; it simplified and strengthened the great administrative departments; and it restricted the Pension List. Public opinion ran so strongly in favour of the bill that Lord North did not dare to oppose it openly; it passed the second reading, but did not survive the Committee stage. When Rockingham came into power in 1782 the bill was re-introduced, but in a greatly modified form, and shorn of some of its most essential and most salutary provisions. In this form it received the royal assent. Burke sat silent throughout the debates, not altogether satisfied with the turn things had taken, but steady in his resolve to make the most of his actual situation, and not to reject an offered reform because he saw a more excellent and thorough way of setting to work.

'Burke's political writing and thinking,' says Matthew Arnold, 'has more value on some subjects than on others; the value is at its highest when the subject is Ireland.' The truth of this comparative estimate might be questioned, but there can be no doubt that the value is very high. The volume in which Arnold has collected Burke's scattered utterances on Irish affairs is one which cannot be neglected by any serious student of Irish history; and one cannot but regret that what Arnold has done for this section of the great orator's work should not have been done by some hand as competent for the whole of Burke's writings and speeches. One of the difficulties in reading Burke is that, in order to gain a complete view of his opinions on the great questions to which he devoted his life, one has to hunt through volume after volume, and to find the object of one's search mixed up with much extraneous matter. There is certainly room for a new edition of Burke, which should proceed on the plan of grouping together his scattered writings in the same or cognate subjects, and furnishing them with such historical introductions as might be necessary to place his readers at the proper point of view from which to judge them. The appearance of such an edition in well-appointed volumes at a moderate cost might give a considerable stimulus to the study of a writer who can hardly be too much studied, and who is at present grievously neglected. In these days when writers of not a tenth part of Burke's calibre, and works dealing with subjects of infinitely less importance, are edited with a care and fulness which not seldom err on the side of excess, it must be a matter of extreme surprise and regret that such an edition should still be a desideratum.

The history of Ireland since the first English adventurers landed on its shores makes one of the saddest pages in our annals.   It is a history of successive conquests and confiscations, of spasmodic and impotent revolts followed by cruel measures of repression.   The unhappy natives were persecuted for their tenacity in holding fast to their ancient religion; they were denied all participation in the government of their country, and shut out by monstrous laws from the most ordinary privileges of citizens.   It will be profitable under Burke's guidance to examine a little in detail the various parts of this atrocious system.

As Burke points out (*Letter to Sir Hercules Langrishe*, 1792), 'the Revolution (of 1789) operated differently in England and Ireland in many, and these essential, particulars. . . . In England it was the struggle of the great body of the people for the establishment of their liberties against the efforts of a very small faction who would have oppressed them.   In Ireland it was the establishment of the power of the smaller number at the expense of the civil liberties and properties of the far greater part, and at the expense of the political liberties of the whole.'   The race hatred between the English settlers and the native Irish was intensified by a bitter religious feud.   The inevitable results were written in the statute-book of an exclusively Protestant Parliament.   The Catholics were , excluded, under the Popery Laws, from holding any office under the Crown. The parliamentary franchise was denied them. No Catholic could be a legal practitioner even of the lowest rank. Peculiarly monstrous provisions had the effect, as Burke shows (*Tracts on the Popery Laws*) of setting children against their parents and wives against their husbands, and further, of discouraging all industry and frugality. Successive confiscations had put nearly all the landed estates of the country into the hands of Protestants; in order to keep them so Catholics were disabled from purchasing land. The spirit of the same relentless bigotry was seen in the laws which made it illegal for a Roman Catholic to keep a school, or even to teach in a private family; while the system of tests at the Universities shut out the richer Catholics from opportunities of gaining higher education. In these circumstances many parents sent their children abroad to receive the culture which they were denied at home; one finds it hard to believe that even this was forbidden under heavy penalties. Lastly, the natives were taxed to maintain an alien church, while the exercise of their own religious ceremonies was forbidden, and the priests, who to them were the ministers on earth of the Most High, were treated as criminals and outlaws.

While the native Irish thus suffered under the rule of Protestant ascendency, the whole country was sacrificed to the commercial interests of England. Ireland was ground between the upper and nether millstones of Protestant ascendency and English trade jealousy. A great part of Ireland, then as now, was under pasture ; in the interests of English farmers the export of its cattle into England was forbidden. Ireland was suffered to have no share in the trade with the English Colonies. The entrance of its woollens into England was practically prohibited through the jealousy of English weavers and clothiers.

The first step towards the establishment of free trade between the two countries was taken in 1778. We were then engaged in the American War, and it was a matter of supreme importance to conciliate Irish feeling. Lord North introduced a timid and partial measure, which would have removed a few of the restrictions on Irish trade. But hardly had they been introduced when they were abandoned in deference to the loud outcry which was instantly raised by the English merchants. Burke on this occasion took the manly and decided part which might have been expected from his liberal notions of trade, and his strong sympathy with the country of his birth.   Bristol was as loud against the bill as the other commercial centres of the kingdom, and remonstrances, protests, and menaces poured in upon Burke.   To these he replied with admirable spirit and wisdom.   'Do we,' he asked with generous warmth, 'in these resolutions *bestow* anything upon Ireland?   Not a shilling.   We only consent to leave them in two or three instances the use of the natural faculties which God has given to them and to all mankind.'   To allay the fears of the merchants, he pointed to the results which had followed the establishment of free trade with Scotland.   'Such virtue there is in liberality of sentiment that you have grown richer even by the partnership of poverty.'   He showed himself opposed to that old maxim which till Adam Smith's day was the foundation of our commercial policy—the maxim that trade is, not a mutual benefit, but a sort of warfare in which one country can only gain at the expense of another.   'Beggary and bankruptcy,' he maintained, 'are not the circumstances which invite to an intercourse with . . . any country ; . . . it is the interest of the commercial world that wealth should be found everywhere' (*Letter to Samuel Span, Esq.*, 1778).   'I know that it is but too natural for us to see our own *certain* ruin in the *possible* prosperity of other people.   It is hard to persuade us that everything which is *got* by another is not *taken* from ourselves.   It is fit that we should get the better of these suggestions, which come from what is not the best and soundest part of our nature, and that we should form to ourselves a way of thinking more rational, more just, and more religious.   Trade is not a limited thing; as if the objects of mutual demand and consumption could not stretch beyond the bounds of our jealousies.'   'Ireland,' he declared, 'has never made a single step in its progress towards prosperity in which you have not had a share, and perhaps the greatest share in the benefits' (*Letter to Messrs. ******** ****** and Co.*, 1778).   Reason, however, was thrown away on men trembling for their trade privileges, and Lord North, always firm where firmness was misplaced and complaisant where firmness was required, withdrew the measure.   The results which followed were an ample vindication of Burke's action.   For once Protestant and Catholic were united by a common grievance.   The Irish Volunteers, a force formed for the purpose of repelling an anticipated French invasion, assumed a menacing attitude.   The Irish Parliament took a high tone.   As Burke said in a letter to a member of that body, they shortened the credit given to the Crown to six months; they hung up the public credit of the kingdom by a thread ; they refused to raise any taxes, whilst they confessed the public debt and the public exigencies to be great and urgent beyond example (*Letter to Thomas Burgh, Esq.*, 1780).   Lord North was frightened into submission.   As Burke complained, with not unnatural bitterness, the English Government had got into the habit of refusing everything to reason and surrendering everything to force.   His endeavour had been to render by preventive graces and concessions every act of power at the same time an act of lenity—the result of English bounty, and not of English timidity and distress (*Letter to John Merlott, Esq.*, 1780).

The triumph of the Irish Parliament led them to form larger views.   Hitherto that body had been in strict subordination to England, all power of initiating legislation having been taken from it by Poynings' Law.   This supremacy it now resolved to shake off.   England, engaged in a desperate and unequal conflict with America, France, and Spain, was in no condition to resist their claim, and in 1782 the Irish Parliament became entirely independent.   The transfer of the scene of action from Westminster to College Green did not relax the vigilance with which Burke contemplated the struggle of Ireland to work out its own salvation.   Unfortunately no very liberal measures could be expected from an assembly constituted as the Irish Parliament then was. The aid of the Catholics in the struggle for independence was, indeed, acknowledged by a bill which granted them the free exercise of their religion, but at the same time the old oppressive civil disabilities were re-enacted. Burke was emphatic in his disapproval. 'What I could have wished,' he wrote to an Irish peer, 'would be to see the civil advantages take the lead ; the other, of a religious toleration, I conceive, would follow, in a manner, of course. From what I have observed, it is pride, arrogance, and a spirit of domination, and not a bigoted spirit of religion, that has caused and kept up those oppressive statutes. I am sure I have known those who have oppressed Papists in their civil rights exceedingly indulgent to them in their religious ceremonies, and who really wished them to continue Catholics, in order to furnish pretences for oppression. These persons never saw a man by converting escape out of their power, but with grudging and regret. I have known men to whom I am not uncharitable in saying, though they are dead, that they would have become Papists in order to oppress Protestants, if, being Protestants, it was not in their power to oppress Papists.'

It was not until ten years afterwards (1792) that a beginning was made towards admitting Roman Catholics to the parliamentary franchise. In the meantime, Pitt's scheme for complete freedom of trade between England and Ireland came before Parliament. It cannot but be regretted by every admirer of Burke that, under the influence of a purely fanciful analogy between the minister's proposals and the attempt to tax America, he should, in common with the whole Whig party, have resisted this eminently wise and liberal measure. The fact that he now found himself in line with the merchants and manufacturers whose hostility to the measure of 1778 had cost him his seat, ought in itself to have caused him to doubt of the wisdom of his views.

The letter which Burke addressed to Sir Hercules Langrishe in 1792, regarding the admission of the Irish Catholics to the franchise, is one of the finest of all his pieces. It is worth noting that it was written at a time when Burke, according to Mr. Buckle, was 'under a complete mental hallucination.' In his absorption in the struggle against the French Revolution he might have been forgiven a momentary forgetfulness of the wrongs and needs of the country that gave him birth. The letter is ample proof that his mind was as clear and sane, his logic as keen, and

his sentiments as liberal as ever. To the cry of
' The Church in danger,' he retorted that whenever
he should be convinced—which will be late and
reluctantly — that the safety of the Church is
utterly inconsistent with all the civil rights whatsoever of the far larger part of the inhabitants of
the country, he should be extremely sorry for it,
because he should think the Church to be truly in
danger. ' It is putting things into the position of
an ugly alternative, into which I hope in God
they never will be put.' He urged that the Irish
Parliament should show towards the Catholics
a portion of the same magnanimity which the
English had shown in 1782. ' Compare what was
done in 1782 with what is wished in 1792 ; consider the spirit of what has been done at the
several periods of reformation, and weigh maturely
whether it be exactly true that conciliatory concessions are of good policy only in discussions
between nations, but that among descriptions in
the same nation they must always be irrational
and dangerous.' In a keenly ironical passage he
set aside the fears expressed lest the Pope should
gain a footing in Ireland, and become its real
sovereign. He describes the Pope as a ' com-
modious bugbear, who is of infinitely more use to
those who pretend to fear than to those who love
him, and laughs to scorn the idea of him taking

that fierce tyrant, the King of France, out of his jail and arming him with bulls and pardons to invade poor old Ireland, and to force the free-born, naked feet of your people into the wooden shoes of that arbitrary monarch.' The 'naked feet' is a stroke of genius. But he soon laid aside irony, and the passage which immediately follows is as weighty as anything he ever wrote. 'I do not believe,' he proceeds, 'that discourses of this kind are held, or that anything like them will be held, by any who walk about without a keeper. *Yet I confess that on occasions of this nature I am the most afraid of the weakest reasonings because they discover the strongest passions.* These things will never be brought out in definite propositions. They would not prevent pity towards any person; they would only cause it for those who were capable of talking in such a strain. But I know, and am sure, that such ideas as no man will distinctly produce to another, or hardly venture to bring in any plain shape to his own mind, he will utter in obscure, ill-explained doubts, jealousies, surmises, fears, and apprehensions, and that in such a fog they will appear to have a good deal of size, and will make an impression, when, if they were clearly brought forth and defined, they would meet with nothing but scorn and derision.'

Burke's dominant idea was now a dread of the progress of Jacobinism. In a curiously ingenious fashion he contrived to connect his views on that subject with his advocacy of Catholic emancipation. He urged with great emphasis that the surest way to throw the Catholics into the arms of the Jacobins was to continue to exclude them from a share in the constitution.[1] In several curiously characteristic passages he deprecates any attempt to make the Catholics abjure their ancient religion, lest they should become, not Protestants, but atheists. The cause of religion was now menaced, not by the Pope, but by the freethinkers, and it was both unseemly and suicidal for those to whom Christianity was dear to be wrangling over minor details of doctrine and discipline with this grave peril at their door. The events of 1798, the revolt of the United Irishmen and their intrigues with the French, bore emphatic evidence to Burke's sagacity and political prescience. But before those dark days had come the hand of death was laid on the great statesman who had been one of Ireland's wisest, truest, and staunchest friends. The prospect, indeed, looked black enough when Burke passed away, worn out with a life of arduous toil. The

---

[1] See *Letter to William Smith* (1795), and *Second Letter to Sir Hercules Langrishe* (1795).

hopes of the Catholics, which had been raised high by the mission of Lord Fitzwilliam, were dashed to the ground by his recall. Burke had shared those hopes, and an air of despondency hangs over his last utterances on Irish topics. 'Things must take their course,' he said sadly in a letter written only a month before his death.

It is impossible to conjecture with any degree of certainty whether Burke would have approved of the Union. At no time does he seem to have shown himself unwilling to consider its desirability, though his utterances on the subject are cautious and guarded to a degree. It is likely that he would have recognised that the step was forced on Pitt as the one way out of the imbroglio into which Irish affairs had got. He was too well acquainted with the meaner side of politics to have held up his hands with holy horror at Pitt's employment of the only means by which the Union could be brought about. One of the saddest things in the history of Ireland has been the inability of her people to recognise their best friends and their truest patriots, their tendency to heap rewards and honours on those who have sullied her fair fame, to follow with a generous confidence unworthy leaders, and to contemn and neglect those who speak to her in the accents of truth and sincerity. If ever in the fulness of time the eyes of Ireland should be opened—if ever she should cease to fight against the 'nature of things,' and should strive to see things as they really are, the name which she will most of all prize and honour will be that of the great statesman whose love of Ireland was mixed with no base alloy of hatred to England, and whose efforts on her behalf were marked by a sanity, a temperance, and a foresight in which her chosen leaders have, alas! for the most part, shown themselves miserably deficient.

There may be a doubt as to which of Burke's writings possess the most permanent value; there can be none as to which of them have created the keenest interest and caused the widest controversy. That distinction belongs unquestionably to his writings on the French Revolution. Most of the other questions with which he dealt are no longer open questions; the world has long since made up its mind upon them. Some of them were ephemeral in their nature, and now possess merely an historical interest. But that astonishing portent known as the French Revolution is almost universally recognised as the greatest event in the history of modern Europe. It has cast the potency of its spell over the most diverse minds; it has exercised the ablest heads and the most skilful pens of two generations of thinkers. Among the shoal of books on this subject which have issued from the press, Burke's still take a commanding place ; and if Carlyle's *History* is unmatched for its pictorial, dramatic, and picturesque effects, Burke's *Reflections* remains by far the ablest and most philosophical exposition of the view taken by conservative thinkers of the great questions raised in so acute a form by the French Revolution.

We have seen that in 1769 Burke, in his first political pamphlet, had predicted that the deplorable state of the French finances would sooner or later lead to a catastrophe which might involve the whole of Europe. In this he was at one with the most competent observers of the time. Sixteen years before, indeed, Chesterfield had written that all the symptoms which he had met with in history previous to great changes and revolutions in government existed, and daily increased, in France.[1]

The great wars into which the ambition of Louis XIV. had plunged France had brought the nation to the verge of bankruptcy. His successor had to face a task which might have proved beyond the powers of the ablest monarchs known to history; and Louis XV. was one of the most

----

[1] *Letters* : 25th December 1753.

incapable and dissolute sovereigns who had ever
sat upon the throne of France. The need for a
strong and capable monarch was all the greater,
because France, in the midst of modern Europe,
still retained the impress of the feudal organisa-
tion. Louis XIV.'s well-known saying, '*L'état,
c'est moi*,' was no idle boast, but the expression
of a profound truth. The French form of
government was a monarchy of the most absolute kind. Even before the Revolution of 1689
none of the English sovereigns could properly be
described as absolute monarchs. As early as the
fifteenth century, Sir John Fortescue had proudly
called attention to the difference between the
English and French forms of government. One
leading cause of that difference was that in England the nobles had made common cause with
the people in resisting the encroachments of the
Crown. But in France a despotic and highly
centralised system of government shut out even
the nobles from any real share in the conduct of
affairs; they existed merely for show and ornament. The so-called parliaments, with the
parliament of Paris at their head, bore little
resemblance to the powerful body of the same
name in England. In reality their functions
were judicial rather than legislative; their sole
legislative function—if one could dignify it by

that title — consisted in registering edicts presented to them by the king. They had, indeed, won, and occasionally exercised, the right of protesting against these edicts, but if the king chose to disregard their protests, they were powerless to resist his will by constitutional means.

The exclusion of the *noblesse* and the dignified clergy from the direction of the policy of the nation was compensated by the privileges and immunities which partly exempted them from taxation, and placed the greater part of the burden on the shoulders least able to bear it. The mass of the people were still liable to render those feudal services which had been imposed when the conditions of national life were radically different, and which in England had long since disappeared, or been commuted for money payments. The condition of the peasants was deplorable, as one may realise by a perusal of Arthur Young's *Travels in France*. The whole empire, in short, although outwardly presenting an appearance of great splendour and prosperity, was suffering from an inward decay which only the most prompt and vigorous measures could have arrested. It is right to dwell a little on this side of the question, because it is the side on which Burke touches but slightly.

Meanwhile, a great intellectual movement was passing over France like a wave. The eighteenth century was throughout Europe an epoch of immense intellectual activity, and the dominant temper of the great writers of the time was one of restless inquiry and all but universal scepticism. Nowhere, however, was that spirit so widely spread as in France. Nowhere was the play of thought freer, or the spirit of inquiry keener or more relentless. Montesquieu, in his monumental work, had pointedly and vigorously eulogised the British Constitution. Voltaire, with almost incredible activity, sent forth volume after volume in which he applied his admirable literary talents, his keen, rapier-like wit, his agreeable raillery, to discredit existing institutions. But the crowning impulse came from the strange and distorted genius of Rousseau. Montesquieu would have been amply satisfied to see the French Government brought into something like the English form. Voltaire took too cynical a view of human nature to be a democratic leader ; his preference was rather for a benevolent aristocracy. But Rousseau, starting from a theorem that man was inherently and naturally virtuous, and that society was responsible for his vices and crimes, declared himself, in the most unequivocal terms, against property, and argued that no power was legitimate which did not emanate directly from the sovereign people. The startling nature of his paradoxes, and the persuasive eloquence with which he enunciated them, created for him a wide audience; and to the teaching of the *Contrat Social* must largely be ascribed, if not the up-heaval itself, at least the shape into which the revolutionists attempted to mould the government of France.

While this vast intellectual fermentation was going on Louis XV. died, and his grandson, the ill-fated Louis XVI. came to the throne (1774). The new monarch was a mere boy, with a good heart and fair intentions; but he was weak, irresolute, and vacillating. That everything now depended on the personal character of the sovereign is the opinion of such competent authorities as Professor Flint and Mr. Lecky. 'The old order of society,' says Professor Flint, 'could not endure. The only question was, How was it to give place to another? Was it to be through the action of the monarch, or of the people? I see no reason for believing that it might not have been brought about in the former way, that the Revolution in the form which it actually assumed was inevitable, even at the accession of Louis XVI.' He proceeds to argue that if Louis XVI. had been a capable sovereign 'there would have

been no French Revolution like that which
actually happened, no taking of the Bastille, no
"night of Spurs," no September Massacre or
Reign of Terror, and yet all the principles and
strivings which led to the Revolution might have
been as fully realised. *The Revolution may have
no more added to the power or influence of the stream
of thought and tendency which characterises the
eighteenth century, than the cataracts of Niagara
increase the force and volume of the St. Lawrence.*[1]

Unfortunately, Louis XVI. was not such a
monarch. The financial straits of the Government were now extreme, and Turgot, who, soon
after the King's accession, became Controller-
General of the Finances, was driven to propose
that the *noblesse* and the clergy should surrender
their exemption from taxation. Had the King
steadily backed up the great minister, the whole
course of French history might have been changed.
But Louis bent before the storm of indignation which Turgot's schemes provoked, and the
minister was dismissed (1776). The ingenious
schemes of Necker, his successor, did practically
nothing to remove the deficit, and the Government soon after plunged into the American War.
This was a fatal step, for not only did the expenses
of the war saddle France with a new increment of

---

[1] *History of the Philosophy of History in France*, ch. iv.

indebtedness, but the soldiers who took part in it returned to France with a new zeal for liberty, and the example of a purely democratic community across the Atlantic powerfully impressed the public, already disposed towards democracy by the writings of the philosophers. Calonne, a French Townshend, who succeeded Necker, could hit upon no better plan than that of convoking the Notables (1787), and asking them to lay aside their privileges. The only result of this step was to secure his own dismissal. After other fruitless attempts at financial reform, it was decided to convoke the States-General, a body which had not sat since 1614. The elections threw France into a state of violent excitement. As soon as the States-General assembled (May 4, 1789), it became evident that the Third Estate was resolved not to take a subordinate position. Hot disputes broke out as to whether the three Estates should deliberate in common, and these ended in the triumph of the Third Estate. The French Revolution had now begun, and the victory of the Third Estate was quickly followed by the attack on the Bastille (July 14, 1789). Next came the march of the Paris mob on Versailles, and the King and royal family were brought in triumph to Paris.

In England the news of these great events was

at first received with sympathy and approval. Fox, on hearing of the fall of the Bastille, exclaimed, ' How much is this the greatest event that ever happened in the world, and how much the best!' The majority of English politicians regarded the French Revolution of 1789 simply as a counterpart of the English Revolution of 1689; they thought that France was now, thus late in the day, asserting her right to those liberties which England had won a hundred years before. Poetic souls like Wordsworth and Coleridge welcomed the Revolution with a burst of enthusiasm. But Burke from the first regarded the Revolution with hatred and distrust. The only explanation which seems to Mr. Buckle adequate to account for Burke's attitude is that he was suffering from a complete mental hallucination. This reminds one of poor D'Espréménil, whom the National Assembly, says Carlyle, will by and by, to save time, 'regard as in a state of distraction.' To Mr. Buckle the answer must be short. If Burke was mad when he wrote the *Reflections*, the disease was chronic and of long standing. It is no doubt easy, by taking detached passages from his earlier writings, as Lord Brougham has done,[1] to show a seeming

---

[1] *Sketches of English Statesmen in the Time of George III.: Burke.*

inconsistency between these and the tone of thought which permeates the *Reflections.* But a fairer and juster criticism will recognise that Burke attacked the French Revolution on exactly the same principles which he had consistently professed all through his public career. No one has brought this out better than Mr. Morley, who differs widely from Burke in his view of the French Revolution.

Burke was not the man to conceal his opinions because they might be distasteful to his associates. As early as January 1790 he seized an opportunity in the House of Commons for denouncing the Revolution. Fox had eulogised the authors of the Revolution. 'The French,' exclaimed Burke, 'have shown themselves the ablest architects of ruin who have hitherto existed in the world. In a short space of time they have pulled to the ground their army, their navy, their commerce, their arts, and their manufactures.' He now set vigorously to work on his book, and in October 1790 the *Reflections on the French Revolution* was published.

Few books have had a greater influence on political thought, and few so well repay a careful study. To Burke, with his deep-rooted conservatism, his passionate attachment to the past, his hatred of everything in the slightest degree approaching revolution, his distrust of abstract logic, his almost mystic manner of regarding the social structure of a country, the proceedings of the revolutionary party in France were utterly hateful. He regarded all existing institutions, even the most defective, with a sort of super-stitious awe, an awe which sprang from his conviction that they were not the result of mere accident, but of mighty forces acting silently and unseen through countless ages of history. One may imagine how a man, thinking in this way, would regard the destruction at one blow of the whole social system of France. It is important to remember that the *Reflections* were written long before the Revolution assumed its more violent forces, for it shows that Burke's opposition sprang from his hatred to the principles on which the new constitution was based.

The text of the *Reflections* was a sermon by Dr. Price, a Dissenting minister, in which he had praised the Revolution, and extolled its authors for following the example set them by the English a hundred years before. Burke had no difficulty in winning a dialectical triumph over Dr. Price, by showing that the English Revolution had proceeded on traditional and hereditary lines, and that there was no real analogy between the two cases. Perhaps the one weak point in the argument is that Burke seems to overlook the fact that the English Revolution, although it seemed merely to assert the ancient rights and privileges of the people of England which had been violated by James II., in reality involved the transfer of power from the Crown to Parliament.[1] In the congratulations bestowed upon the French for having at last achieved their liberty he refused to join, and he gave his reasons in a weighty passage: 'When I see the spirit of liberty in action, I see a strong principle at work; and this, for a while, is all I can possibly see. . . . I must be tolerably sure, before I venture publicly to congratulate men upon a blessing, that they have really received one. . . . The effect of liberty to individuals is that they may do what they please: we ought to see what it will please them to do before we risk congratulations, which may be soon turned into complaints.' The English form of liberty, he held, was an affair of tradition and inheritance: 'By this means our liberty becomes a noble freedom. It carries an imposing and majestic aspect. It has a pedigree and illustrating ancestors. It has its bearings, and its ensigns armorial. It has its gallery of portraits, its monumental inscriptions, its records, evidences,

[1] I think Mr. Leslie Stephen has a remark to this effect in his *History of English Thought in the Eighteenth Century.*

and titles. *We procure reverence to our civil institutions on the principle upon which nature teaches us to revere individual men—on account of their age, and on account of those from whom they are descended.* All your sophisters cannot produce anything better adapted to preserve a rational and manly freedom than the course that we have pursued who have chosen our nature rather than our speculations, our breasts rather than our inventions, for the great conservatories and magazines of our rights and privileges.' The French, on the other hand, had 'set up their trade without a capital.' Instead of 'heaving the lead every inch of the way,' they had thrown both chart and compass overboard, and voyaged boldly into unknown seas.

One of the most weighty and characteristic passages of the *Reflections* is that in which Burke with equal courage and candour justifies what the Revolutionists called mere prejudices: 'We are afraid to put men to live and trade each on his own private stock of reason, because we suspect that this stock in each man is small, and that the individuals would do better to avail themselves of the general bank and capital of nations and of ages. Many of our men of speculation, instead of exploding general prejudices, employ their sagacity to discover the latent wisdom which prevails in them. If they find what they seek—and they seldom fail,—they think it more wise to continue the prejudice with the reason involved, than to cast away the coat of prejudice, and to leave nothing but the naked reason ; because prejudice, with its reason, has a motive to give action to that reason, and an affection which will give it permanence. Prejudice is of ready application in the emergency ; it previously engages the mind in a steady course of wisdom and virtue, and does not leave the man hesitating in the moment of decision, sceptical, puzzled, and unresolved.' Prejudice renders a man's virtue his habit, and not a series of unconnected acts. Through just prejudice, his duty becomes a part of his nature.'

The great fault of the *Reflections* is that Burke refused to recognise the evils of the old system of government. He would admit nothing that was urged against the conduct and character of the nobles and the clergy. To see the other side of the shield, one must turn to Carlyle and Taine. The old *régime* was doomed—doomed by its own faults and vices.

As the Revolution assumed a more violent form, Burke's indignation steadily increased. In his *Letter to a Member of the National Assembly* we have the first intimation of that crusade against the Revolution which he was to devote the rest of his life to preaching.

Burke was violently reproached by the Whigs who followed Fox with apostasy from all the principles he had formerly professed. He replied in *The Appeal from the New to the Old Whigs* (1791)—a calm and masterly vindication of his absolute consistency. In balance, in serene mastery of his facts, in symmetry and proportion, this book must rank very high among Burke's efforts.

A reaction now rapidly set in against the French Revolution. When the more violent spirits obtained the upper hand, and the execution of the King was resolved upon and carried out, war between the two countries was inevitable. Burke, however, was emphatic in his disapproval of the way in which the war was carried on, and in his *Letters on a Regicide Peace* he put forth all his powers to ensure its continuance in a more determined fashion. We do not recognise the better part of Burke in these letters; vituperation has taken the place of argument, and one can only marvel to what excesses of passion the wisest of statesmen can allow himself to be carried. In magnificence of declamation, however, nothing in Burke surpasses the *Letters on a Regicide Peace*, and the irony of the fourth Letter is unique of its kind.

Burke now felt that his days on earth were drawing near a close. The stage had darkened ere the curtain fell. The death of his son had been a grievous blow to a man whose domestic affections were as strong as his political passions. He was filled with the most gloomy forebodings of the fate of Europe. A darker moment was, indeed, yet to come, when the dying Pitt, pointing to a map of Europe, was to say, 'Roll up that map; it will not be wanted these ten years.' But the outlook was black and gloomy enough; the French were carrying everything before them, and the whole Western world was veiled in thick battle-smoke, when Death brought Burke's career of beneficent activity to an end, July 9, 1797. He had barely reached the allotted span of threescore and ten; but he had never thought of sparing himself, and the severe strain of his manifold activities had told in the end upon his constitution. In the nature of things, the toil of a statesman can rarely be of that blessed sort described by the poet as 'toil unsevered from tranquillity'; he must count himself happy if he may look for his recompense to the gratitude and admiration of posterity. To that gratitude and that admiration no statesman possesses a stronger or surer claim than Edmund Burke.

MATTHEW ARNOLD[1]

IT is not my intention in what follows to write a life of Matthew Arnold, but rather a criticism of his work. Indeed the materials are not at hand for an essay of the former kind, as no biography of Arnold has yet appeared. It will suffice, therefore, if I note at the outset that Matthew Arnold, the son of Dr. Arnold, the famous head-master of Rugby School, was born in 1822; that he was educated at Rugby, Winchester, and Oxford; that as one of Her Majesty's Inspectors of Schools he did good service to the cause of secondary education; and that he also held for a time the post of Professor of Poetry at Oxford. Finally, his death, at the age of sixty-six, so recently as 1888, will be fresh within the memory of all. With this hasty sketch of a life outwardly, at least, uneventful, I pass to the more immediate purpose of this essay.

The difficulty in dealing with an author who has produced so much and such varied work as Matthew Arnold is to know what to select and

[1] Heriot-Watt College Literary Society, February 1892.

where to begin. I choose to begin with his poetry, for this reason : If one set out to inquire what is the current idea of Matthew Arnold—in what light the mass of readers chiefly regard him, one would find, I think, that very few would fix upon his poetry as that which constitutes his chief significance in their eyes. Yet to those who wish well to Arnold's fame, his poetry has a very special value ; in his poetry his chief significance for them does really rest. For it is perhaps the only portion of his work which is genuinely creative, and only work which has this character can hope to live. No doubt we value his other books very highly ; to us, to our generation, they have been fresh and fascinating, they have been inspiring and stimulating, in a very high degree ; and so, I trust, they will be for some generations to come. Nevertheless, they are merely critical, not creative ; they belong, that is to say, to what is after all a fugitive form of literature, and so they cannot be regarded as safe. Time goes on, new problems spring up, a new criticism engages men's minds, and names that once were great become as the mere shadow of a shade ; nay, the very triumph of the critic's ideas acts, in the end, to the detriment of his fame. But all the while work which has this character of genuine creation abides, does not pass, becomes a last-

ing possession of the race. So I say that those
who think highly of Arnold do well to put
his creative work in the foreground ; and this
creative work is found in his poetry more than
anywhere else.

Fortunately, when we thus fall back on Arnold's
poetry we fall back on something the strength
and excellence of which gives us good reason to
hope that it *will* so survive, that it *will* become a
lasting possession of the race. Arnold's limitations, indeed, are many and evident. What is
perhaps the supreme poetical gift of all, the lyrical faculty—the power, that is, of the free, direct,
spontaneous utterance of an emotion, a passion, at
once common, fresh, and deep—this supreme gift
he can hardly be said to possess at all. His voice
is not naturally rich and full ; his lines rarely
haunt one with their unique melody. He is
essentially a meditative poet; in him, as in
Wordsworth, there is an excess of the contem-
plative and brooding spirit over the passionate.
Wordsworth's influence, indeed, we could very
easily trace in Arnold's poetry, even if we did not
know from himself how strong that influence was.
His fine tribute to Wordsworth's memory will no
doubt be familiar. Speaking of the deaths of
Byron, Wordsworth, and Goethe, those three
great heroes of his, he says :—

> 'Time may restore us in his course
> Goethe's sage mind and Byron's force ;
> But where will Europe's later hour
> Again find Wordsworth's *healing power?*
>
> He laid us as we lay at birth,
> On the cool, flowery lap of earth ;
> Smiles broke from us, and we had ease ;
> The hills were round us, and the breeze
> Went o'er the sunlit fields again ;
> Our foreheads felt the wind and rain.
> Our youth returned, for there was shed
> On spirits that had long been dead,
> Spirits dried up and closely furled,
> The freshness of the early world.'

Yet as strong as was Wordsworth's influence over him, his culture and his humour saved him from Wordsworth's great mistake—the mistake of confounding what is common with what is merely commonplace. The passion of love, for instance, is a common one ;—I speak without experience in these matters, but I suppose we might describe it as a universal passion ;—yet it is never commonplace—to those interested, and to the poet, —and therefore it is eternally a fit subject for poetry. A red-haired man is also common, but he is not on that account a fit subject for poetry. So, also, a donkey is a common and an unobjectionable animal ; still one does not expect the best sort of poetry to occupy itself with donkeys. Wordsworth forgot this ; hence *Peter*

Bell and *The Idiot Boy*, and all the rest of
that tiresome company, hence also their lineal
descendant, Mrs. Leo Hunter, in the *Pickwick
Papers*, with that plaintive little lay of hers about
the expiring frog. On the other hand, Arnold
never quite reaches the altitude to which Wordsworth occasionally attains ; such a line as

' The light that never was on sea or land.'

is quite out of the younger poet's power. In
short, comparing these two, it is quite safe and
quite correct to say, that of inspiration Arnold
has far less than Wordsworth, of culture he has
far more.

The bulk of Arnold's poetry, as I have indicated, is reflective. Yet some of his finest work
is to be found in narrative poems like *Sohrab
and Rustum* and *Balder Dead*, in semi-dramatic
poems like the *Sick King of Bokhara* and
Empedocles on Etna. In these his classic mode
of treatment shows itself strongly—in the easy
strength of the verse, in the engaging simplicity
of touch, in the fine felicity of diction, but most
of all, in his grand austere, impersonal way of
treating things. We are not so much impressed
by particularly fine passages as by the artistic
completeness, the rounded perfection, of the
whole. The total effect is grand ; yet, precisely

for this reason, it does not do to pick out isolated passages. From this class of his poems, therefore, I content myself with only one quotation. For exquisitely clear, sweet, lucid word-painting, it would surely be hard to beat this passage from one of his earliest poems, *Empedocles on Etna*—

> ' Far, far from here,
>   The Adriatic breaks in a warm bay
>   Among the green Illyrian hills ; and there
>   The sunshine in the happy glens is fair,
>   And by the sea, and in the brakes.
>   The grass is cool, the seaside air
>   Buoyant and fresh, the mountain flowers
>   More virginal and sweet than ours.'

It was that passage, prefixed by Charles Kingsley to one of the chapters of *Alton Locke*, which first led me to the study of Arnold's poetry ; and I have loved it ever since.

We enter a different world altogether when we come to deal with Arnold's reflective poetry—a world of doubt, of melancholy, of unrest. Here, more emphatically than anywhere else in literature, is pictured that struggle between the old faith and the new reason which plays so tremendous a part in the intellectual life of our day. For Arnold, as for so many more to-day, the old faith had lost—not indeed its charm, for that remained, but—its hold over his mind. He felt that if Christianity was to remain a power for good, it must be transformed; and he did not very well see how this transformation was to be brought about. Hence that melancholy — that 'sad lucidity of soul,' as he has so finely phrased it— which is the dominant note in his reflective poems. He describes himself as

> 'Wandering between two worlds, one dead,
> The other powerless to be born.'

Yet it is a melancholy which holds its head high; he is resolute not to falter with his reason, not to admit illusions, however enticing.

> 'Because thou must not dream, thou need'st not then despair.'

To the promptings of despair he opposes a proud resolution, an unconquerable though sad serenity. He holds firmly by Goethe's great principle of resolute self-dependence; he insists on the fact of the essential solitariness of the human soul, on the fact that each one of us has in truth to work out his own salvation. In a famous stanza he declares—

> 'Yes, in the sea of life enisled,
> With echoing straits between us thrown,
> Dotting the shoreless watery wild,
> We mortal millions live—alone.'

Between even the nearest friends there rages, he says, in one of his grandest lines,

> 'The unplumb'd, salt, estranging sea.'

K

And dwelling thus alone, we have to study our own mind and follow its best promptings.

'No man,' he says,—

> 'No man can save his brother's soul,
> Or pay his brother's debt.'

And again :—

> 'Once read thy own breast right
>   And thou hast done with fears ;
> Man gets no other light,
>   Live he a thousand years.'

And then, as a relief to these feelings, he turns constantly to another of his great primary themes, the silence of nature and its calm, 'its toil unsevered from tranquillity.' One is constantly coming across descriptive passages, to the full as clear, simple, and lucid as the one quoted, and after the weariness and languor which so often go before, one rests in these passages with a feeling of joy and satisfaction.

From what I have said one may gather that Arnold's poetry is never likely to become popular, in the wide sense of the word. It is cold with the coldness of Milton's later style, the style of *Paradise Regained* and *Samson Agonistes*. Enthusiasm and passion Arnold did not readily feel and he does not readily awake; the mass of readers will always probably be left cold by his poetry as they are left cold by *Samson*

Agonistes. But to those who are readily responsive to the classic note in poetry, Arnold comes closer perhaps than any other of our poets; and by such his memory will always be held in honour. Gravity and dignity of thought, a firm and sure grip of his subject, rare and choice gifts of expression, an uncompromising austerity of treatment, an exquisite sense of form and proportion, these are never absent from his verse; they give it that tone of conscious distinction which marks it all; they make it classical; they raise it to the level of an art which is both fine and true. It is work, one emphatically pronounces, which will stand the test of time well; in it there is nothing spurious, nothing unworthy. For Arnold, it has well been said, 'the essentials were dignity of thought and sentiment, and distinction of manner and utterance.' And therefore, despite its limitations, his poetry may surely be allowed to rank with that best poetry regarding which he said that 'it will be found to have a power of forming, sustaining, and delighting us as nothing else can.'

As a poet Arnold was—and is—overshadowed by Tennyson and Browning; but during his lifetime he was allowed on all hands to have the finest critical sense among the men of our time. Arnold was a born critic, and in addition he had the best possible training. His culture was altogether beyond the common run, even among men of letters ; the writers of Greece and Rome, of France and Germany in particular, were as familiar to him as those of his own land. So little insular, indeed, is the general tone of his criticism, that he has been called the most un-English of Englishmen ; he has been said to be far more of a Frenchman than of an Englishman. And unquestionably this is true in a sense. He had, in an eminent degree, that love of lucidity and order, alike in conceptions and in their expression, which characterise the writers of ancient Greece and modern France, although it is to be noted that his Teutonic birth asserted itself in the greater gravity and seriousness of his views of life. Excess or extravagance of any kind he abhorred, he could not away with. He felt and acknowledged, for instance, the regal supremacy of Shakespeare, but he would none of Shakespeare's ways ; for himself, he went back and found his truest inspiration and best model in the classical writers of antiquity. Now it is important to bear this in mind when we read his literary criticism, for it explains a good many things. It explains, for instance, the slight store he set by Shelley's poetry. Not only did he rate it as of small value, but he actually hazarded the prediction that Shelley's essays and letters would in time come to stand higher than his poetry. And if his hatred of excess and extravagance led him to undervalue Shelley, it led him also to overrate such a poet as Gray. 'Gray,' he said, 'is one of our classics; the scantiest and frailest of our classics, it is true, but still a classic.' Now, although I am well aware how universal is the condemnation of Johnson's estimate of Gray in the *Lives of the Poets*, I really think Johnson comes nearer the truth; in fact, what I have to find fault with in Johnson's Life of Gray is not its wrong-headed judgment, but its egregious bad taste. He treats Gray as if he were a charlatan or an impostor, and whether Gray is one of our classics or not, he certainly was not that. Macaulay quotes with censure Johnson's description of Gray, expressed in conversation, as a barren rascal; but really, making allowance for Johnson's way of expressing himself, that epithet 'barren' does not seem far from the truth. If we bear in mind, then, this tendency of Arnold's, and if we also remember that he is sometimes inclined to be over-fastidious, we could not have a safer or a better guide to the real enjoyment of the master-pieces of literature.

A safe guide Arnold generally is; he is always a fascinating and delightful one. His prose style is simply one of the most delightful in the range of our literature. It flows so freely and so easily ; it is so admirably flexible, so clear, so lucid, so simple in construction, yet so fine in its effects. It ranks with Addison's as the finest example we have of the well-bred colloquial style of prose—a style differing, indeed, from ordinary, cultured conversation, having a slight exaltation of tone that such conversation has not, but differing less from it than it does from the *mechanical* style of such writers as Johnson and Macaulay. It was his constant command of an admirable style, in conjunction with his natural sense of what was fine in literature and what was not, which enabled him to produce such critical masterpieces as, to mention no others, the essays on Heine and Marcus Aurelius in the first series of *Essays in Criticism*, and those on Wordsworth and Byron in the second series. His style is really his own, in every part, even to his love of quotation and of repetition. No great writer whom I have read quotes so freely as Arnold ; and no great writer repeats himself so often. His constant custom was to take some wise and pregnant saying uttered by some famous personage like Plato, or St. Paul, or his favourite Bishop Wilson, and to make this the text, as it were, of his discourse ; to walk all round it, to amplify it, to enlarge it, to

come back to it again and again. So dexterous
is the use he thus makes of quotation, that one
cannot find it in one's heart to blame him for
being too prodigal in its employment. So, too,
his endless repetitions of himself are all in-
tentional, and it was in fact by dint of this
practice that so many of his phrases have become
popular and current. Still, it is a habit which is
occasionally irritating ; as, for instance, when he
repeats the phrase 'Scotch religion, Scotch drink,
and Scotch manners' four times within the compass of a single page. One cannot but remark,
also, in his prose the fine tone of irony of which
he can on occasion make so terribly effective a
use. His tone is perfectly courteous, but the
irony is all the keener because it *is* so perfectly
courteous. He is an expert swordsman, who, with
a bland smile on his countenance, is through his
adversary's body before he quite realises what
has happened. The very gravity and seriousness
with which he states his opponent's case has
sometimes all the force of irony. 'Mr. James
Gordon Bennett says that the highest achievement
of the human intellect is what he calls "a good
editorial." *This is not quite so.*' That is all, but
—poor Mr. Gordon Bennett !—what comment
would be more caustic, more quietly incisive than
that? Again, in how exquisitely ludicrous a

light he contrives to place the cry for the displacement of the classical in favour of modern languages, when he tells us that he was 'brought up at Oxford in the bad old times, when we were stuffed with Greek and Aristotle, and thought nothing of preparing ourselves, by the study of modern languages, to fight the battle of life with the waiters in foreign hotels!'

If any one wishes a very fine example of Arnold's prose style at its best, let him turn to the beautiful apostrophe to Oxford in the preface to the first series of *Essays in Criticism.*   Oxford, 'the home of lost causes and forsaken beliefs, and unpopular names and impossible loyalties.'   Or again, there is that fine passage, charged with an unusual animation and fervour, in which, seizing on the significance of Byron's work as a revolutionary element in English society, he exclaims : ' His own aristocratic class, whose cynical make-believe drove him to fury, the great middle class, on whose impregnable Philistinism he inevitably shattered himself to pieces—how little have either of these felt Byron's vital influence !   As the inevitable break-up of the old order comes, as the English middle class slowly awakens from its sleep of two centuries, our actual present world to which this sleep has condemned us shows itself more clearly— our world of an aristocracy materialised and null,

a middle class purblind and hideous, a lower class
crude and brutal,—we shall turn our eyes again
and to more purpose upon this passionate and
dauntless soldier of a forlorn hope, who, ignorant
of the future and unconsoled by its promises,
nevertheless waged against the conversation of
the old, impossible world so fiery battle, waged it
till he fell, waged it with such "splendid and imperishable excellence of sincerity and strength."'

'The great middle class, on whose impregnable
Philistinism he shattered himself to pieces'—'a
middle class purblind and hideous,' these phrases
may fitly serve to introduce us to another side
of Arnold's work—his praise of culture, his plea
for more sweetness and more light. In the first
place, then, let us see what Arnold exactly means
by Philistinism. This he has told us very clearly
in the preface to his admirable book on the *Study
of Celtic Literature.* 'On the side of beauty and
taste, vulgarity ; on the side of morals and feeling,
coarseness ; on the side of mind and spirit, unin-
telligence—this,' he says, 'is Philistinism.' And
he goes on : 'Far more than by the helplessness
of an aristocracy whose day is fast coming to an
end, far more than by the rawness of a lower class
whose day is just beginning, we are imperilled
by what I call the Philistinism of our middle
class.'

Now, I think we ought to have a notion what sort of a person our Philistine is. But to make quite sure, let me try to sketch his portrait. He is, then, a very respectable, very serious, and very stupid person, who lives only to make money and achieve respectability; who cannot, therefore, be properly said to live at all. With great ideas he has absolutely no commerce; he lies entirely outside the current of the 'best that is thought and known in the world.' His politics are provincial, and so is his religion,—provincial in their limited outlook, their lack of breadth and freedom. He rarely reads, and he never thinks; but, on the other hand, he usually has a balance at the bank, and he always carries an umbrella. His ideas are ignoble; his whole way of life, petty, uninteresting, even hideous. The serious business of his life is money-making; his amusements, political and sectarian agitation, tea-meetings, and, at the present moment, listening to Messrs. Moody and Sankey. Of course he has a library; for, after all, books are furniture, and if books are not dear to your Philistine's heart for their own sake, furniture is. But his books are not for reading; they are to be shown to admiring friends, to be carefully dusted and as carefully left unread. If he reads at all, his great literary hero is the author of *Self Help*, that great and glorious monument of complacent commonplace, which no country but our own could have produced,—that grand expansion of what Arnold called Mrs. Gooch's Golden Rule, or the Divine Injunction, 'Be ye Perfect' done into British. 'Ever remember, my dear Dan,' Mrs. Gooch used to say every morning to her son when he was starting for work,—'Ever remember, my dear Dan, that you should always look forward to being one day manager of that concern.' And 'my dear Dan' *did* remember it, and, behold! he became wealthy, and died Sir Daniel Gooch. And then Mr. Smiles came and played Mrs. Gooch's part on a grand scale; he produced that masterpiece of his with the express purpose of showing how, if one only reads *Self Help* and goes to bed early, and gets up at four o'clock in summer and five in winter, he will of a surety become the manager of whatever concern he happens to be engaged in. And verily Dr. Smiles hath his reward; for has not *Self Help* gone through I don't know how many editions, and is it not the book beyond all others best beloved of the British Philistine's heart?

This, then, is the Goliath against whom Arnold waged incessant warfare. He never tired of this theme. Again and again he took up his parable against the narrowness, the illiberality of English middle-class life. He insisted that this Philistin-

ism, with its absorption in petty cares, its want of
high ideals, its complete and debasing self-satis-
faction, was damaging and hurtful in the last
degree to every side of our national life ; and the
grand remedy for it lay, he said, in culture—a
culture which should infuse more sweetness and
more light into the lives—the dreary, hideous lives
—of those around us.   The culture he meant was
not that false sort which is so often confounded
with it, and which no doubt is fair game for the
scoffer,—it is not, I say, that false sort which
plumes itself on a little knowledge of Greek and
Latin.   No, it is, in Arnold's own words, 'an
endeavour to get at the best that is thought and
known in the world, to propagate that best,
and, by so doing, to turn a current of new and
fresh ideas on our stock notions and habits.'
That is what Arnold meant by culture, and those
who fully seize the significance of what that
means will be chary, I think, of underrating the
efficacy of such a process.

Still, in order that the process may be effica-
cious, the concurrence of the Philistine is necessary, and this is precisely where Arnold failed.
That he did fail was not, however, his own fault,
but that of the Philistine.   In the first place,
he did not buy Arnold's books; if he *had*
bought them he wouldn't have read them ; if he

had read them he wouldn't have recognised his own portrait ; and if he had recognised his own portrait he wouldn't have cared in the least. For against dulness the gods themselves do battle in vain, and, luckily for his peace of mind, your Philistine is dull—dull with a dulness portentous and awe-inspiring.

At the same time, it would not be fair to leave our friend the Philistine without saying that Arnold recognised to the full his good points— his honesty in walking by the best light he has, his good humour, his sincere sense of the vital importance of religion. And perhaps, also, it is well after reading Arnold to turn, for instance, to Mr. J. M. Barrie's books, so full of wise and tender observations—to turn, let us say, to *Auld Licht Idylls*. The life so admirably depicted there is narrow enough in all conscience ; it has never been touched with culture. If these Thrums people were only wealthy, one has a presentiment that they would be Philistines to a man. Yet with how much of humour and pathos has Mr. Barrie contrived to invest these grim and gaunt figures ! But after doing this justice to the Philistine, let us repeat once more that his is not an ideal life ; that it is hard, that it is narrow ; and that the nobler ideal is the one which Arnold sets before us.

When Arnold came to deal with religion and

the Bible, as he does directly in *Literature and Dogma* and one or two more of his books, indirectly and incidentally in nearly every one of them, he started out with two propositions. The first of these was that we cannot do without Christianity; the second was that we cannot do with it as it is. Those of you who have read his books do not require to be told how strong Arnold's love of the Bible was, how fully he recognised the fitness of its teaching to be in truth the rule of our lives. Here, then, he broke with those who are for putting the Bible aside altogether as antiquated and out of date; but when he came to apply his second proposition he broke no less decisively with the upholders of orthodox religion. Arnold claimed for himself and for others the right to deal with the Bible just as freely as with other books, to submit it to the same tests, to apply to it the same standards. To those who find themselves able to take everything in the Bible quite literally he did not address himself; with them he did not seek to meddle. Nor did he appeal to those who dismiss the whole affair as altogether unworthy of credence, or even of serious consideration. He wrote for those who, like himself, knew and loved the Bible, but who, like himself again, could not bring themselves to do that violence to their reason implied in taking all the statements in the Bible as matter of fact, and who in consequence were in doubt and perplexity as to their course in regard to these great and sacred matters. He wrote for those who felt that, in its reliance on miracles and the supernatural, Christianity was on untenable ground, on ground which it must sooner or later abandon, unless its power over men's minds was altogether to pass away.

To this great and growing class of persons Arnold addressed himself. He said frankly that the retention of miracles was impossible, that the Bible miracles could not be placed in a class by themselves, that the miracles *in* the Bible must inevitably go the way of the miracles *out* of the Bible, that the only effect of their retention was to hinder and not to help Christianity. He said, further, that a great portion of the Bible was to be regarded as poetry, not as science, not as matter of fact; that, regarded as science, much of its language could have for us no sense of reality; regarded as poetry, it remained grand and beautiful. But popular Christianity had taken this poetical language and treated it as if it were scientific; it had taken this fluent language and made it hard, rigid, definite, and out of it had constructed formulas, had elaborated and built up creeds.

But these creeds and formulas men were beginning to look upon with distrust and aversion, and the danger was that in the growing discredit which was befalling them the grand and vital realities of the Bible would be discredited also. To prevent this, it was necessary, he said, to abandon the supernatural, and to fall back on the natural truth of Christianity—its natural truth as proved by the experience of men and the history of nations. The real message of the Old Testament was this—'Salvation by Righteousness'; the real lesson of the New Testament, 'Righteousness by Jesus Christ.' The Enduring Power, not ourselves, which makes for righteousness—this, he said, was the God of the Old Testament. No doubt the Old Testament writers put into their conception of God more than this ; no doubt they made Him what orthodox religion still makes Him—namely, a magnified and non-natural man. But this conception of Him as the Enduring Power, not ourselves, which makes for righteousness they had ; and this is a real and substantial conception, while the other is not verifiably that. It is easy, no doubt, to object that this definition of God is a vague one ; and no doubt that is so. Only, it must instantly be rejoined that Arnold would not have considered that an objection at all ; for one of his charges against orthodox and popular religion is that it is too definite by far, where it has no right to be definite; that it professes certainty where from the nature of the case certainty is not possible; that after saying in one breath that God is altogether beyond the reach of our thoughts, it calmly goes on in the next breath to talk as if He were a man living in the next street, with the workings of whose mind we were perfectly acquainted.

And so, as regards the New Testament, its grand purpose is, he says, the revelation of Christ. Our business is not with those speculations about His miraculous birth and His miraculous resurrection, which are so vain and so idle, it is not with that admiration of His life, which is so cheap and so easy; no, it is with that imitation of His example, which is so costly and so difficult, and withal, of such immense and supreme importance. The miraculous elements in the Gospels are to be regarded simply as lovely and beautiful legends, as accretions which inevitably grew up in that far-off time round the story of a life such as that of Christ—the life of One who was so far above the heads even of His disciples, that they could not fully comprehend or adequately report Him.

That is a sketch of Arnold's religious views, as full as my limits permit. His influence on religious thought has been great; it has been felt even by those who most bitterly attacked him. Dogma is being discarded bit by bit; there is a growing aversion to dwelling on the supernatural side in the Bible; everywhere the personality of Christ is more and more being put in the foreground. But that such a transformation as he desired to see is still necessary, is evident enough. Look, for instance, at the present position of our own Free Church. Those of you who have been following the controversy over that precious Declaratory Act, with its 'compromises' and 'holy ambiguities,' will, I think, hold very lightly in future creeds, confessions, and such like documents, as not worth the paper they are written on. Surely the Free Church will require to learn—all the Churches will require to learn—that in truth there is something singularly uncompromising; that in ambiguity there is nothing 'holy,' but something quite the reverse. One can only look with pity at the two parties in this controversy— the one party strenuously striving, with evident sincerity and good faith, to uphold doctrines and creeds which can serve man's turn no longer; the other party trying to patch up, out of compromises and holy ambiguities, something that may pass muster for a year or two, something that may last out *their* time. What can we say of the one set, but that they are striving, vainly and ineffectually striving, with that current against which nothing can strive successfully, the current of time? And of the other set what can we say, but that they are drifting, slowly and reluctantly, but none the less surely, drifting with the tide, instead of striking out vigorously for themselves?

My survey of Arnold's literary work, incomplete and inadequate on many sides as I am well aware it is, must now have an end; it remains for me to add a word or two as to the personality of this most fascinating and engaging of writers. Many are the testimonies to the charm of his conversation, to the grace and ease of his manners; to his deeper qualities of mind and heart—those qualities by which all men must at last stand or fall— let me call just one witness. 'Than Matthew Arnold,' wrote Lord Coleridge, soon after his friend's death, 'few souls ever passed away with more hope of acceptance, few lives more unstained have been led from childhood to old age, few men have ever gone into that silent void where, if there are no smiles, there are no tears, and where, if hearts do not beat, they cannot be broken, leaving behind them such passionate regrets, such daily, hourly desire for communion which the grave forbids, for friendship which Death has ended.' That is the testimony of one who knew him well; it is what every one who reads his books, and is fascinated by them, will like to believe, and will find it easy to believe. To my mind, the figure of this man has a grace and charm which belong to only one or two in the whole history of our literature—to Sir Philip Sidney, to Edmund Spenser, to Joseph Addison ; his memory, like theirs, is of sweet savour, his name, like theirs, of sweet sound. Through all the controversies of his time he passed with temper unruffled, with mind unclouded and serene ; he worked hard, harder by far than most men, yet, in his own fine phrase, his toil was ever 'unsevered from tranquillity.' And so we seem to see him, with that lofty brow and look of serene triumph, passing away in the consciousness that he had laboured for ideals that were lofty and true, that he had guided his own course well, and helped others to guide their course well also, that to the best of his power he had borne his part in the attempt—the necessary, the noble attempt—to usher in a type of man, 'more intelligent, more gracious, and more humane.'

A. C. SWINBURNE [1]

I

THE last seven years have seen three great lights
of later English poetry go out one by one. In
1888 Matthew Arnold, that fine genius who had
shed so clear and steady a radiance over wide
tracts of thought and feeling, died four years before he had attained the allotted span of threescore and ten. Robert Browning followed next,
leaving behind him a mass of the richest poetic
ore, imbedded, alas! in the roughest quartz, and
requiring the vigorous use of pick and spade
in order to be come at. Last of all, in the ripe
fulness of his years, but in the unabated exercise
of powers which seemed ever to be gaining new
breadth and vigour, Alfred Tennyson was taken
from us, with an exquisitely beautiful swan-song
on his dying lips. To those who value the great
traditions of English song, it seemed as though
the poetic sky was 'dispeopled now and void,' as
though with the removal of these three great

[1] President's Essay to the Heriot-Watt College Literary Society,
October 1895.

figures we declined upon a race of lesser men.　I
do not know that we were greatly consoled when
Mr. Traill came forward with his list of fifty
minor poets—an allowance of the bread perhaps
rather more than adequate.　But when the first
shock of their lamented deaths was over, we
began to reflect with thankfulness that though
much was taken much was left, and that we had
still in our midst one or two poets not unworthy
to be ranked but a little below the great men who
had passed.　Mr. William Morris, indeed, has
long since forsaken the banner of the Muses to
hold aloft the red flag of Socialism; but Mr.
Swinburne remains faithful to his art, and still
pours out his exuberant vitality with the same
force and freshness as of old.　It is of this singer,
in whom all competent judges recognise the only
successor of the late Laureate, that I wish to
write with what measure of power I possess.

It is almost exactly thirty years since Mr.
Swinburne dazzled and enchanted the reading
public with his first great poem.　There are poets
who go from strength to strength, to whom the
years bring a deeper and wider vision, and a
richer and more significant music, poets whom we
begin by calling exquisite and end by calling
sublime; of these, the most highly favoured sons
of Apollo, Shakespeare is the standing example.

There are others who concentrate their best work within a few crowded years of their life, and who in the periods on either side of this glorious harvest-time produce work infinitely inferior: Wordsworth will occur to every one as a notable representative of this less favoured order. There are poets who seem to shoot up all at once to maturity, and who never afterwards rise greatly above or sink greatly below the high level to which they had at first attained. It is to this class that Mr. Swinburne indubitably belongs. If we set aside poems so obviously unripe, though in parts of great beauty and abundant promise, as the *Queen-Mother and Rosamond*, and regard *Atalanta in Calydon* as the first exquisite fruit of his mature Muse, then we are forced to say that Mr. Swinburne has never done anything better, if indeed he has done anything quite so perfect, as this poetic drama, which he published in 1864 at the age of twenty-seven. This fact would of itself absolve me from the necessity of following the chronological order of his works, since the sole advantage of that method in the eyes of all save pedants lies in the clue it affords to the growth and development of an author's genius. Mr. Swinburne, besides, has been so fertile that it would be impossible for me, within my limits, to make much more than bare mention

of all his works. I must content myself, therefore, with a very general survey of his poetry.
This very copiousness is often urged against Mr.
Swinburne as a reproach ; and there is a sense in
which the complaint has some shadow of justifica-
tion. It is important, however, to see clearly what
that sense is. No one will be so foolish as to say
that fecundity in itself is other than a virtue, as the
sign of a soil naturally rich and exuberant. When
a writer is culpably careless, when he produces a
vast mass of work, much of which is slovenly,
slipshod, down-at-heel, we may indeed reason-
ably wish that he had written less, and taken
more pains to make it perfect. Byron in poetry
and Scott in prose undoubtedly lay themselves
open to this charge. Wordsworth, again, is a
poet who pays the penalty of over-copiousness
by being often dull, prolix, flatly prosaic. Now,
Mr. Swinburne can certainly be charged with
neither of these sins. He is copious, but he is
never careless ; the artistic instinct is so deeply
ingrained in his nature, that we may be sure no
work ever leaves his hand until it is as perfect in
its kind as he can make it. Undeniably prosaic,
again, he never is ; the bogs and marshes and
flat, shifting sands of Wordsworth's worst work
have no counterpart in Mr. Swinburne's poetry.

What, then, do Mr. Swinburne's critics mean

by reproaching him with a too lavish prodigality? They mean that the superstructure of his poetry does not rest upon a broad enough foundation; that his verse is not sufficiently informed with thought. They cry out, 'O monstrous! a ha'porth of bread to this intolerable deal of sack.' They assert that the magnificence of his verbal music cannot long blind us to his lack of ideas, and that he drowns his meaning beneath a torrent of what only the impetuous rush and the splendour of the diction prevent them from describing as sheer verbiage. Language, the old cynical saying has it, was given to man to enable him to conceal his thought; language, one of Mr. Swinburne's severer critics would say, has been given to him to conceal his lack of thought. Obviously we are here confronted with what is one of the most difficult and hotly contested questions in literature—the relative importance, namely, above all in poetry, of form and substance. I do not therefore think any apology necessary for trying to see at some length how the case actually stands. Suppose, then, we put the question in this form : Can we have fine poetry which is yet almost wholly divorced from ideas?

The fugitive and elusive nature of the charm which poetry lays upon our minds is sufficiently attested by the very fact that no adequate or final definition of poetry has yet been hit upon by the ingenuity of poets and critics. Coleridge's definition of it as 'the best words in the best order' is refreshingly simple and unpretentious, but obviously it does not take one very far. More ambitious attempts have invariably been failures more or less complete. Shelley's definition is one of the best: he describes poetry as the expression of the best thoughts of the best moments of the best minds. Wordsworth's definition, 'Emotion recollected in tranquillity,' characterises his own poetry admirably, but breaks down lamentably when applied to poets of a more passionate and less meditative cast of mind than the sage of Rydal. My present purpose will best be served by scrutinising a definition still more famous and widely current than any of these. Matthew Arnold said, and (*more suo*) repeated till the public had got the phrase firmly fixed in their minds, that all literature is a criticism of life, and that poetry is a criticism of life made in conformity with the laws of poetic truth and poetic beauty. Well, that has a very philosophical air, and we naturally look with great interest to see how the critic applies his theory. Fortunately, as I think, for the soundness of his criticism, but unfortunately for the authority of his definition, we find that he uses the term 'criticism of life' in a sense so large, vague, and elastic, that it ceases to have any real significance. When, for example, we find him assuring us that 'when Keats utters a moral idea,' with the line 'For ever wilt thou love and she be fair,' we are forced to conclude, either that our guide is making fun of us, or that the phrases 'criticism of life,' 'moral ideas,' have an entirely strange meaning on his lips. Again, in his fine essay on Keats, Arnold tells us that Keats had a magical felicity in rendering the charm of nature, but that for the interpretation of the moral side of man he was not ripe—a declaration which one of Arnold's 'plain men' would naturally consider as equivalent to saying that Keats had no criticism of life to offer. Yet Arnold quotes the modest remark of Keats, 'I think I shall be among the English poets after my death,' and adds the emphatic comment, 'He is; he is with Shakespeare.' The truth would appear to be that Arnold, consciously or unconsciously, had to choose between Keats and his definition, and that he wisely preferred to make the less precious sacrifice. My own position I must make as clear as I can in a few rapid sentences.

I think then we might profitably distinguish between three different orders of poets. In the first and supreme order we observe the union of high intellectual power, profound imaginative grasp on the realities of life, and serious and noble feeling, with an intense love for beauty, and a gift of so touching the chords of human speech as to render the spell of that beauty potent on our minds. Such a union is one of the rarest things in the world; when it does take place we have a poet such as Shakespeare. But when we descend to a lower plane, we find poets in whom these qualities are no longer united in perfect equilibrium and harmony. The balance now leans to this side or that; some have as ardent a love for the beautiful as Shakespeare, but are weak on the reflective side; with others exactly the reverse is the case. Let us take, for example, two extreme types, and see how they stand in these respects; let us contrast the poetry of Keats with the poetry of the late Robert Browning. Clearly the strength of Keats lies in his devotion to the principle of beauty, and in his incomparable felicity in evoking the charm which lies in words; his weakness, again, lies in the fact that this devotion is with him so absorbing, that it occupies him to the almost entire exclusion of everything else. Robert Browning, however, is strong precisely where Keats is weak, and weak where Keats is strong. On the purely intellectual side Browning is perhaps the richest and most prodigally gifted of our poets except Shakespeare — that terrible Shakespeare whom we can never get behind or above. In all relating to the intellect Keats is a mere child by his side; but then, on the other hand, Browning hardly seems to prize beauty or seek for it; certainly he does not prize or seek for it in anything like equal measure with Keats. He forsakes the lute and the lyre and the shepherd's pipe for the trumpet, and if he often discourses with a clear, ringing and resonant accent, he not seldom falls into the harshest discords and dissonances. I have sometimes thought of likening his poetry to a drive in a springless cart over a rough, uneven road in the midst of a fine country. The prospect, indeed, is commanding and magnificent, but we hardly think of that in the exceeding discomfort of the journey. Or again, one might say of Browning that he is a great poet without those qualities we are apt to think of as distinctively poetical. By that I mean that while by no possibility can we conceive of Keats being other than a poet, we have not the same assurance of certainty in the case of Browning.

Well, we have made a pretty wide circuit, but I think we have got something that will help us in judging Mr. Swinburne. In the first place

I should say : 'Enjoy poetry without seeking to define it ; leave definitions to the men of science. But if you must have a definition, you are bound to make it wide enough to include both a poet such as Browning and a poet such as Keats.' And next, the consideration of the case of Keats leads to the conclusion that poetry may be almost entirely divorced from reflection and yet remain fine art—fine, if not exactly grand or sublime. I think that this would hardly require to be argued, were it not unfortunately the case that a great many very respectable persons, not only read poetry but, actually delude themselves into the belief that they enjoy it, who are yet absolutely deaf to the charm of its music, and absolutely blind to its sweet and subtle suggestions. And so when they come to criticise poetry—if their criticism ever gets beyond the inarticulate stage —they must weigh everything in their moral scales, and introduce considerations which are merely impertinent and irrelevant.

I do not wish to press the analogy between Keats and Swinburne too far. On the one hand, Mr. Swinburne has certainly a wider range of ideas than Keats in his too brief life gave evidence of; on the other, Keats presented the few ideas he had with far more clearness and definiteness of outline. And this suggests the extent

to which I can go with Mr. Swinburne's critics.
The defect of his copiousness is that it is often
hard for us to penetrate through his many-
coloured mist of words to the thought which
these hide rather than reveal, which may be a
virtue in a politician, but which is a vice in a
poet. An attempt, indeed, has been made to
justify this practice by analogy with the art of
music. Undoubtedly we may listen with delight
to fine music, which yet conveys no definite idea
to the mind. Still I think the musician has his
own province and the poet has his, and that no
charm of sound can quite wholly excuse blurred
outlines and vague, treacherous fogs, through
which we wander, ignorant of our goal, with
halting and uncertain footsteps. Let us, then,
go back to our three orders, and see how we
should place Mr. Swinburne. We cannot, I
think, rank him with those with whom a profound
reflective faculty goes hand in hand with the
noblest gifts of expression. The purely artistic
faculty dominates in him over the turn for reflection ; that is to say, he comes far closer to Keats
than either to Shakespeare or to Browning. For
good and evil alike, however, he belongs to the
class of artists pure and simple less decisively
than Keats ; he has not quite that rounded perfection of loveliness which fascinates us in the

best poems of Keats, but he has a wider outlook upon life, and a deeper sense of its profound significance.

But here another set of Mr. Swinburne's critics would chime in with the remark that it is not the limited range of his ideas they object to, so much as the wrong-headed perverseness of such ideas as he has. Alike in morals, in politics, and in religion he goes wildly astray. He has not, they say, a 'well-regulated mind.' To those who pin their faith to that latest monstrosity of sham science, the theorem of the insanity of genius, this will seem merely equivalent to saying that Mr. Swinburne is a poet; for my own part, I am a firm believer in the supreme and radiant sanity of genius. I hold it to be as absurd to say that every madman is a genius, as that every genius is a madman. I am therefore shut out from disposing of Mr. Swinburne's ethics in the curt and easy way which would be open to the disciples of a doctrine so consoling to the average man, who, after reading the treatise on 'Degeneration,' thanks Heaven that he is not as other men, even as those geniuses.

I remarked at the outset that in point of art Mr. Swinburne had never improved upon his first great triumph. His changes of mental attitude, however, have been considerable; or rather, it would be more correct to say that at successive stages of his life the motives which have impelled him to the work of production have been widely different. In discussing the quality of his thought, it will therefore be necessary to distinguish these stages.

In 1866, two years after *Atalanta*, Mr. Swinburne published a volume which one hesitates whether to call famous or notorious, the memorable first series of *Poems and Ballads*. Its appearance was followed by one of those *acute attacks of epidemic morality* which Macaulay satirised so pungently in his essay on Byron. Mrs. Grundy, the British Matron, Paterfamilias, a Disgusted Reader, and all the rest of that pleasant family, at once seized upon the volume with that avidity with which, oddly enough, they read everything to which the least suspicion of immorality attaches, and immediately proceeded to go into hysterics over it. The echoes of that storm of insult and contumely which burst over Mr. Swinburne's head have hardly died away yet, which must be my excuse for making a candid statement of the impression the volume makes on my own mind.

I approach literature with no prudish bias. I dissent completely from that theory, so widely current in our own country, that the supreme

praise with which one can crown a work of art is
that it would not raise a blush to the check of
Mr. Podsnap's Young Person ; rather I think that
the Young Person is an unmitigated nuisance,
and that no work really great can be done by
men who have the fear of that portentous
phantom constantly before their eyes.   The
nursery and the boarding-school may very well
have a literature of their own—from which, by
the way, if Mrs. Grundy were consistent, she
would banish Shakespeare and the Bible,—but do
not let us set up the ideals of the schoolroom as
the standard to which all artists must conform.
So much by way of a general confession of faith.
Let me say now that I do not find Mr. Swinburne's
tone in this volume wholly free from offence.
Freedom of speech is the inalienable birthright of
a great artist, but he must beware lest liberty
degenerate into licence.   The tone of Shakespeare's *Venus and Adonis* is not the tone of
Othello ; in the latter there is no lack, certainly,
of plain and blunt speaking, but this does not
leave even the slightest stain upon the purity of
one of the noblest creations of the human spirit.
Now, Mr. Swinburne offends, as Shakespeare
offends in his early poem, by dwelling too much
on the joys and pains of the senses. His tone,
indeed, is not that of gay and thoughtless liber-

tinism; the nod and wink and leer of the professional Don Juan have no place in his pages. In the reaction against the injustice with which he was treated, some generous critics, indeed, went so far as to say that the tendency of the volume was severely moral, since if he painted in vivid colours the fascinations of sense, he recognised no less plainly, and painted no less vividly, the self-disgust and bitterness in which they end. So far as that I cannot go in his defence; not only would the argument justify the vilest excesses of realism, but it appears to overlook the vital distinction between the tone of grave moral reprobation, and the tone of a wearied-out and disillusioned sensuousness.

What justly offends us is the low conception of the passion of Love. Let me quote, not from the *Poems and Ballads* but, from one of the magnificent choruses of *Atalanta*, a passage which will at once give an idea of Mr. Swinburne's poetic powers almost at their highest, and of this lack of recognition on his part of the higher forms of the passion. The chorus is based upon the old legend of the birth of Venus:—

> ' What hadst thou to do being born,
> Mother, when winds were at ease,
> As a flower of the springtime of corn,
> A flower of the foam of the seas ?

For bitter thou wast from thy birth,
    Aphrodite, a mother of strife ;
For before thee some rest was on earth,
    A little respite from tears,
    A little pleasure of life ;
For life was not then as thou art,
    But as one that waxeth in years,
    Sweet-spoken, a fruitful wife ;
        Earth had no thorn, and desire
No sting, neither death any dart ;
    What hadst thou to do amongst these,
        Thou, clothed with a burning fire,
Thou, girt with sorrow of heart,
    Thou, sprung of the seed of the seas
As an ear from a seed of corn,
    As a brand plucked forth of a pyre,
As a ray shed forth of the morn,
    For division of soul and disease,
For a dart and a sting and a thorn ?
What ailed thee then to be born ?

Was there not evil enough,
    Mother, and anguish on earth,
    Born with a man at his birth,
Wastes underfoot, and above
    Storm out of heaven, and dearth
Shaken down from the shining thereof,
    Wrecks from afar overseas,
    And peril of shallow and firth,
        And tears that spring and increase
In the barren places of mirth,
That thou, having wings as a dove,
    Being girt with desire for a girth,
        That thou must come after these,
That thou must lay on him love ?'

Five years after the *Poems and Ballads* Mr.
Swinburne sent forth *Songs before Sunrise*, a

volume in which he appears as a political propagandist of the fieriest type. Dr. Johnson's opinion of the political and religious creed expounded in *Songs before Sunrise* would no doubt have been expressed in very terse and vigorous English, but one might parody the rather curious eulogium pronounced by the Doctor on one of his friends, and say of Mr. Swinburne that 'he hates a fool, and he hates a king, and he hates a priest: he is a very good hater.' It is on Napoleon III. and last—Napoleon the Little, as Hugo called him— that the vials of his fiercest wrath and deepest scorn are poured forth; he rarely spares him a gentler epithet than worm or dog, and he pursues him into the grave, and beyond it, with implacable hatred and astonishing wealth of invective. The *Songs before Sunrise* are dedicated to the glorification of Republicanism. I cannot say that either the abstract idea of Republicanism, or its concrete embodiment as we see it in France and America, seem to me to have any great charm for the mind or any great sustenance for the spirit. But no matter what we think of Mr. Swinburne's politics, one cannot but admit the almost terrible power of the volume which has so sweet a title. Mr. Swinburne's wrath expresses itself in words that seem almost to burn the page on which they are written. Two things honourably distinguish

Mr. Swinburne from the herd of poets who have sung the praises of liberty. One is that with him the praise of freedom is not a mere piece of conventional clap-trap; the other is the cosmopolitanism of his sympathy. Mr. Swinburne's religious views seem to be curiously compounded out of sheer Paganism and a vague Pantheism. He thinks he sees the Churches associated with the perpetuation of intolerable injustice, and he does not care to distinguish between the essential and eternal truths of Christianity and the corruptions with which it has been overlaid. The specifically Christian virtues of meekness and humility of spirit are not those he prizes most, or seeks to cultivate. I may say frankly that I do not like or admire the bitter, clamorous, and railing tone in which he speaks on such subjects, that I think him often wanting in reverence; but let me add, that so long as the beauty of holiness is obscured by the pitiful ugliness of mere respectability, so long as the Churches cling to creeds in which God shows as a malignant divinity rather than as a beneficent Father, they need not be surprised if a poet of fiery and ardent temperament turns upon them and rends them.

Some one once wrote a book on snakes. One of the chapters was entitled 'Of Snakes in Iceland,' and consisted of these words: ' There are no snakes in Iceland.' After my exposition of Mr. Swinburne's opinions some of you may be inclined to say : 'There are no ethics in Mr. Swinburne's poetry.' What I think would be juster is to say that he does not lay sufficient stress upon the negative virtues. Without entering into the vexed question of the relation between art and morality, might one not suggest that the lack of self-mastery, which is Mr. Swinburne's defect on the moral side, is closely allied to his artistic defects? Perverse and wrong-headed I shall not attempt to deny that Mr. Swinburne often is by his froth and foam and verbiage. Let us at all events not bear too hardly upon the faults of a poet dowered in such ample measure with 'the hate of hate, the scorn of scorn, the love of love,' a poet in whose spirit there is so much that is high and heroic and magnanimous, and nothing that is mean or base or cowardly.

In considering Mr. Swinburne's poetic style, I shall not attempt to discuss in detail its special characteristics. I should perhaps rather say his styles, for what strikes one most is his marvellous power of assimilating style, without, however, losing for a moment his own strongly marked individuality of tone and touch. In command over the most widely diverse metrical forms he has probably no rival in English verse. Among the higher and more arduous forms of poetry there is hardly one in which he has not achieved a more or less unqualified triumph. His genius, indeed, is rather too diffusive for the drama, too little capable of concentration and the rigid exclusion of the superfluous. Throughout the trilogy which covers the whole history of Mary, Queen of Scots—that beautiful and tragic figure who has cast so potent a spell over his imagination—the action halts and limps, while the characters deliver speeches of unconscionable length, although often of marvellous beauty. *Bothwell*, for example, alone occupies something like five hundred pages, and no fewer than sixty-three personages encumber rather than fill its stage. But if his plays bear little evidence of profound insight into character and the secret springs of conduct, they are admirable considered as dramatic poems. Often Mr. Swinburne seems, in his romantic dramas, to catch the very accent of the Elizabethans. Where, for example, are the pains of exile described more poignantly, or with a greater measure of that felicity and charm of diction which we think of as peculiarly Elizabethan, than in the lines I quote :—

'Not death, not bonds, are bitterer than his day
 On whom the sun looks forth of a strange sky,
 Whose thirst drinks water from strange hands, whose lips

Eat stranger's bread for hunger ; who lies down
In a strange dark and sleeps not, and the light
Makes his eyes weep for their own morning, seen
On hills that helped to make him man, and fields
Whose flowers grew round his heart's root ; day like
    night
Denies him, and the stars and heirs of heaven
Are as their eyes and tongues who know him not.'

If in the region of romantic drama Mr. Swinburne has in some respects come as near the Elizabethans as a modern may hope to come, he has achieved a still more unquestionable triumph in the plays which he has modelled on the severe lines of Greek tragedy—the two superb dramas, *Atalanta* and *Erechtheus*. What makes the supreme distinction of these poems is their magnificent lyrical choruses, with their rolling waves of pealing sound, their exultant and impetuous rush. Mr. Swinburne has a fondness for using lines longer by many syllables than is usual in English verse—so long, indeed, that in less skilful hands they would be unwieldy and lumbering. But with him the breadth of his pinions merely accelerates the speed of his flight. In *Erechtheus*, for example, how the lines leap and flash like swords in battle! What other poet could paint a battle-scene in language like this, could so set before us the ' brilliance of battle, the bloom and the beauty, the splendour of spears ' :—

' For now not in word but in deed is the harvest of spears
    begun,
And its clamour outbellows the thunder, its lightning
    outlightens the sun.
From the springs of the morning it thunders and lightens
    across and afar
To the wave where the moonset ends and the fall of the
    last low star.
With a trampling of drenched red hoofs and an earth-
    quake of men that meet,
Strong war sets hand to the scythe, and the furrows take
    fire from his feet.
Earth groans from her great rent heart, and the hollows
    of rocks are afraid,
And the mountains are moved, and the valleys as waves
    in a storm-wind swayed.
From the roots of the hills to the plain's dim verge and
    the dark loud shore,
Air shudders with shrill spears crossing, and hurtling of
    wheels that roar.
As the grinding of teeth in the jaws of a lion that foam as
    they gnash
Is the shriek of the axles that loosen, the shock of the
    poles that crash.
The dense manes darken and glitter, the mouths of the
    mad steeds champ,
Their heads flash blind through the battle, and death's
    foot rings in their tramp.
For a fourfold host upon earth and in heaven is arrayed
    for the fight,
Clouds ruining in thunder and armies encountering as
    clouds in the night.
Mine ears are amazed with the terror of trumpets, with
    darkness mine eyes,
At the sound of the sea's host charging that deafens the
    roar of the sky's.

White frontlet is dashed upon frontlet, and horse against
    horse reels hurled,
And the gorge of the gulfs of the battle is wide for the
    spoil of the world.
And the meadows are cumbered with shipwreck of chariots
    that founder on land,
And the horsemen are broken with breach as of breakers,
    and scattered as sand.
Through the roar and recoil of the charges that mingle
    their cries and confound,
Like fire are the notes of the trumpets that flash through
    the darkness of sound.
As the swing of the sea churned yellow that sways with
    the wind as it swells
Is the lift and relapse of the wave of the chargers that
    clash with their bells ;
And the clang of the sharp shrill brass through the burst
    of the wave as it shocks
Rings clean as the clear wind's cry through the roar of
    the surge on the rocks :
And the heads of the steeds in their headgear of war, and
    their corsleted breasts,
Gleam broad as the brows of the billows that brighten the
    storm with their crests,
Gleam dread as their bosoms that heave to the ship-
    wrecking wind as they rise,
Filled full of the terror and thunder of water, that slays as
    it dies.
So dire is the glare of their foreheads, so fearful the fire of
    their breath,
And the light of their eyeballs enkindled so bright with
    the lightnings of death ;
And the foam of their mouths as the sea's when the jaws
    of its gulf are as graves,
And the ridge of their necks as the wind-shaken mane on
    the ridges of waves :

And their fetlocks afire as they rear drip thick with a
    dewfall of blood
As the lips of the rearing breaker with froth of the man-
    slaying flood.
And the whole plain reels and resounds as the fields of
    the sea by night
When the stroke of the wind falls darkling, and death is
    the seafarer's light.'

That is a passage in which Mr. Swinburne's lyrical fire flames out in a blood-red splendour. For the sake of contrast, and to give a notion of his versatility, let me set beside it one or two verses of a little poem which since I read it has haunted me with its unique melody, its note of brooding pathos, of tender and regretful reproach. The poem is entitled *Itylus* and the speaker — I quote from Mr. William Rossetti—is Philomela, the nightingale, whose love, and the perennial pathos of her sorrowing, reproach her sister Procne, the swallow, in memory of the horrible fate dealt by that sister's hand to her own son Itylus :—

'Swallow, my sister, O sister Swallow,
    How can thine heart be full of the spring?
    A thousand summers are over and dead.
What hast thou found in the spring to follow?
What hast thou found in thine heart to sing?
    What wilt thou do when the summer is shed?

'Sister, my sister, O soft light Swallow,
    Though all things feast in the spring's guest-
        chamber,
      How hast thou heart to be glad thereof yet?
For where thou fliest, I shall not follow,
    Till life forget or death remember,
      Till thou remember and I forget.

     .   .   .   .   .

'O sweet stray sister, O shifting Swallow,
    The heart's division divideth us.
      Thy heart is light as the leaf of a tree,
But mine goes forth among sea-gulfs hollow,
    To the place of the slaying of Itylus,
      The feast of Daulis, the Thracian sea.

     .   .   .   .

'O Swallow, sister, O rapid Swallow,
    I pray thee sing not a little space.
      Are not the roofs and the lintels wet?
The woven web that was plain to follow,
    The small slain body, the flower-like face,
      Can I remember if thou forget?

     .   .   .   .

'O sister, sister ! thy first-begotten !
    The hands that cling and the feet that follow,
      The voice of the child's blood crying yet,
" Who hath remembered me, who hath forgotten "?
    Thou hast forgotten, O summer Swallow,
      But the world shall end when I forget.'

'The words of Mercury are harsh after the songs of Apollo,' and with that exquisite music lingering in our ears I am fain to bring this section of my essay to a close. To characterise Mr. Swinburne's genius in a sentence, I should say that as a wearer of the regal purple of god-like speech, in imaginative ardour and intensity, if not in imaginative breadth and depth, in pomp and magnificence of verbal music, and in the passionate and exultant expression of lyric fire and rapture, he need fear no comparison with even the supreme masters of English song. This is his special merit, and this is his crowning praise.

II

Full as the volume of Mr. Swinburne's poetry is, he has yet found time to make many fruitful excursions into the field of prose. I own to a special fondness for the reading of good literary criticism, finding in it a delight second only to that which I take in the study of the masterpieces of creative art; and it is to this department that Mr. Swinburne has practically confined himself in his prose writings. If his critical work does not count for much in the popular estimate, it is partly because his fame as a poet has justly enough overshadowed his fame as a critic, and partly because of certain faults of temper and method which I shall have to notice later on. The roll of those who in this country have applied themselves seriously to the business of literary criticism is not a long one, and the quantity of critical work of the highest order which we possess is inconsiderable compared with that which some other nations—France, for example—can show. And on that account alone there is reason for rejoicing that a writer of Mr. Swinburne's standing should have devoted some attention to this neglected sphere of literary labour. The volumes of collected essays, and the separate monographs on Shakespeare, Blake, Chapman, and, of course, Victor Hugo which he has sent forth, constitute a very notable and a very welcome addition to our rather scanty stock of fine critical work. The old false and absurd notion that a poet is not the best—if, indeed, he be not the worst—authority on his own craft, can hardly, one would think, survive the discredit cast upon it by the fact that two of our greatest Victorian poets, Arnold and Swinburne, stand also in the very front rank of critics. I am no poet, and I could not, without passing sentence on myself—a task always unpleasant, and here quite gratuitously unnecessary—maintain the converse of this proposition, and assert that, as ' Who drives fat oxen should himself be fat,' so we must look only to the poets for the criticism of poetry ; but of the two it is certainly the more reasonable and credible opinion. Mr. Swinburne's instinct as a critic seems to me by no means unerringly right ; but when all possible deductions are made, there remains much in his matter which is precious and admirable, much that is fortifying and stimulating in his manner. Before examining some of his critical judgments, let me say a few words regarding his prose style.

When Mr. Swinburne ceases to sing, he does not permit us to forget that he is a poet : unfortunately it is often of his weak rather than his strong side as a poet that his prose reminds us. The faults of his prose are those of his verse, and they are faults which of course are less pardonable in prose than in poetry. His diction is far too riotously exuberant; he runs up too broad a canvas of words for the wind of his thought to fill. He is never nerveless or languid ; on the contrary his sins are on the side of over-emphasis, of excess and extravagance. There is nothing like a sense of humour for keeping literature sane and sweet, and I am inclined to ascribe to Mr. Swinburne's signal and regrettable lack of the precious and saving quality those ludicrous excesses and asperities into which he is too often betrayed. I remember only one stroke of humour in all his books, and that, I am afraid, is quite an unconscious one. I refer to a passage in which he speaks of himself as one of those 'who desire above all things to preserve in all things the golden mean of scrupulous moderation '—a claim which I fear will move most of his readers to derisive laughter. I give but a single instance of a fault which must be either painfully or ludicrously familiar to all students of Mr. Swinburne. Some unhappy and misguided mortal has ventured, greatly daring, to insert a word in the text of Shelley's poems, and Mr. Swinburne's wrath bursts forth in this fashion : ' A thousand years of purgatorial fire would be insufficient expiation for the criminal on whose deaf and desperate head must rest the original guilt of defacing the text of Shelley with this most damnable corruption.' After this, who shall say that the Boythorn of *Bleak House* is a caricature? It is well to know on such admirable authority what is the eighth deadly sin, but one cannot but speculate how the respectable Mr. Bowdler would have fared had *he* come under the lash of Mr. Swinburne's castigation. We may admire and enjoy Mr. Swinburne's prose if we read it a few pages at a stretch ; if we sit long over his essays, the stress and glare of his style, its cloying richness, end at last by fatiguing and exasperating us, so that it is a relief to turn to some writer less studious of violent effects, less fond of strong and high colouring.

To mark clearly and fairly faults like these is part

of the ungracious duty of a sober critic. I have
been the more careful to bring them into relief,
because I proceed to make a claim on behalf of
Mr. Swinburne's prose which some of my hearers
may be unwilling to admit. Now that Arnold,
Pater, and Stevenson are dead, and Mr. Ruskin is
all but silent, I do not know of any living writer
who can match Mr. Swinburne at his best, if we
leave Mr. George Meredith out of account as
being too unequal, too freakish, and too fantastic.
He has not the even and equable tone of Arnold,
his consummate and unfailing felicity of phrase,
and he has not Stevenson's subtle dexterity of
craftsmanship, his choice and curious research for
the one word that will fit his purpose. Compared
with any of these I have mentioned, Mr. Swinburne's style seems heavy and overloaded. Yet
he is the master of some stops on the organ of
prose which it did not enter into their scheme to
use.   In amplitude and sonorousness, in grave
and rich fulness of musical cadence, in pomp of
golden-tongued eloqence, we must, to find fit
rivals for him, go back to that earlier age when
such qualities as these were held in higher esteem
than the virtues of simplicity, lucidity, and direct-
ness, which we now look for and praise in
English prose.   I like Mr. Swinburne best when
he writes in the minor key: no ear can surely be dull

to the subdued and restful beauty of the passage
on Shakespeare's Prince Arthur which I quote:
' I am not minded to say much of Shakespeare's
Arthur; there are one or two figures in the world
of his work of which there are no words that
would be fit or good to say. The place they have
in our lives and thoughts is not one for talk;
the niche set apart for them to inhabit in our
secret hearts is not penetrable by the lights and
noises of common day. There are chapels in the
cathedral of man's highest art, as in that of his
inmost life, not made to be set open to the eyes and
feet of the world. Love and death and memory
keep charge for us there, in silence of some
beloved names. It is the crowning glory of
genius, the final miracle and transcendent gift of
poetry, that it can add to the number of these,
and engrave on the very heart of our remembrance
fresh names and memories of its own creation.'
To call this merely eloquent would be to do it
wrong: it is eloquence breathed upon by the
breath of a born poet.

III

Within the limits fixed by a high standard of
excellence Mr. Swinburne's taste is admirably
catholic. He has flung himself into the study of

letters with that fiery ardour which marks all he does, and he has brought to bear upon his task not only the ripe knowledge of a finished scholar, but that unfeigned love of all that has been grandly or finely done in art, and that swift insight into the secret of its triumphs without which all criticism is doomed to failure.   The radical defect of his critical method is that he almost invariably forces the note; his praise passes too often into fulsome flattery, his censure into shrill vituperation.   I do not think that he often praises work wholly unworthy, or that he often fails to make his repugnances at least intelligible.   Whether he praises or blames, he is apt to scatter his superlatives with far too lavish a hand.   If there were a tax on the luxury of superlatives—a measure I recommend to the consideration of any potential Chancellor of the Exchequer here present,—Mr. Swinburne would find the demands on his purse rather heavy.   He is too apt to be

> 'So over-violent or over-civil
> That every man with him is god or devil.'

Victor Hugo might stand for the supreme god of his literary idolatry, and Thomas Carlyle for the devil.   To speak seriously, I cannot think that Mr. Swinburne in his praise of Hugo has gone to work in the winning and persuasive way. He should lay to heart the old fable of the Wind and the Sun and the traveller's cloak. There is no doubt something touching and attractive in his lifelong devotion and loyalty to Victor Hugo, and certainly to recommend the great men of one nation to one's fellow-countrymen is a noble and praiseworthy task. But it is a task which must be gone about with more circumspection than Mr. Swinburne has shown. Had he not pitched his tone of eulogy quite so high, he would not only have come far nearer the truth about Hugo, but he would actually have served him better with a class of readers whom his extravagant and unmixed adulation merely wearies and repels. I hope I have a becoming reverence for the greatest figure in French literature, but surely there is hardly a great writer whom we must accept, if we accept him at all, with so many reserves and hesitations, so that it requires the recollection of his astonishing merits to outweigh the sum of his grievous offences against art. Hugo's lack of balance and measure, his love of startling paradox, the frequency with which he crosses the line that separates the language of passion from the language of sheer rant—these are faults which Mr. Swinburne consistently ignores. Hugo, as I have said before, is a giant who must perpetually be straining upon tiptoe: let me add now, that his natural stature is so great that he does not require to stand upon the prostrate bodies of his admirers. Mr. Swinburne's praise of Victor Hugo would have counted for far more in the estimate of all thoughtful readers, had he not so persistently clapped the telescope to his blind eye when Hugo's faults came within the range of his vision.

Victor Hugo looms largest in Mr. Swinburne's essays, but he is far more than a mere Hugolater. His *Study of Shakespeare* is a noble and eloquent tribute to the memory of one in writing of whom it grows hard to avoid the obvious without making excursions into the irrelevant. Mr. Swinburne, indeed, is perhaps the first living authority on that glorious Elizabethan literature which we all praise, but which so many of us know so little about. He has followed worthily in the wake of Coleridge and Lamb, by directing attention anew to the 'large utterances of those early gods.' Shakespeare Mr. Swinburne views mainly on the purely poetic side of his genius, a manner of approaching him which I find refreshing and salutary after the portentous efforts of those German commentators who, by the aid of a vast and cumbersome apparatus of learning, discover all sorts of wonderful things in Shakespeare which Shakespeare never dreamt of putting there. Towards the great poets, his contemporaries and rivals, Mr. Swinburne is singularly and nobly free from the least taint of jealousy or envy. When we are tempted to bear hardly upon his asperities of temper, let us remember to his credit that large generosity and noble magnanimity of nature to which his tributes to Tennyson, Arnold, Browning, Morris, and Rossetti bear ample and eloquent witness. When the late M. Taine, in one of those too frequent aberrations of the critical sense which make his *History of English Literature* one of the most exasperating, as it is by far the most brilliant, study of our literary monuments, set Alfred de Musset above Tennyson, Mr. Swinburne was one of the first to utter an emphatic protest. I do not agree at all points with Mr. Swinburne's estimate of the late Laureate ; I certainly go with him in his condemnation of the whining heroics of *Locksley Hall* and the unreal sentiment of the *May Queen*, but I cannot, even at his bidding, give up the *Idylls of the King* which Mr. Swinburne nicknames the ' Morte D'Albert, or Idylls of the Prince Consort.'

Mr. Swinburne breathes freest in the atmosphere of controversy ; he loves ' to drink delight of battle with his peers.' In Matthew Arnold he encountered a foeman worthy of his steel, and there is no more vigorous piece of critical polemics than the essay on Wordsworth and Byron in which Mr. Swinburne contested the high claims put forth on their behalf by Mr. Arnold, and asserted the counter-claims of his own favourite Shelley. I cannot enter into the merits of that great debate ; the honours of the field were pretty equally distributed between the two champions, and neither, perhaps, was entirely in the right. I can merely express, without any attempt at proof, my opinion that Mr. Swinburne's estimate of Shelley is as extravagantly high as Arnold's was extravagantly low, that to Byron he is in many respects unjust, and that of Wordsworth he writes with a measure of sympathy and insight greater than I should have expected or hoped for from him, considering the widely diverse temperaments of the two men. To settle questions of precedence, to act as a sort of Burke's Guide to the Intellectual Peerage, is not to my way of thinking the main function of criticism ; but of course such questions have an interest of their own. I take it that at present the star of Wordsworth is manifestly waxing, while that of Byron is no less manifestly waning, and Shelley gains but little ground. All attempts to re-habilitate Byron will, I am afraid, be utterly

futile; he can never recover the place he held in
his own generation, although a candid criticism
will always recognise in him more than, to use
Swinburne's over-emphatic language, 'rant and
cant and glare and splash and splutter.' Shelley,
on the other hand, is so impalpable and elusive,
that he is perhaps doomed to be the poet of a
select circle of devout votaries; but Arnold's
astounding prediction that his essays and letters
would in time come to rank higher than his
poetry is likely to remain unfulfilled. Of the
three, Wordsworth, by virtue of that power which
Mr. Swinburne has so accurately defined as
'sublimity in tenderness,' has perhaps the surest
and firmest hold on the affections of that inconsiderable minority of persons who take any vital
interest in the great achievements of art, and no
revolutions of time or taste will displace that
serene and august figure from the pre-eminence
he has so fairly and worthily earned.

IV

In bringing this far from complete study of Mr.
Swinburne to a close, I am happily able to
express the feeling with which I take my leave
of him in words fitter and more beautiful than
any I could write. In his charming preface to

Men and Books Mr. Stevenson says of the authors he there deals with—how admirably, the readers of the volume know: 'These were all men whom for one reason or another I loved ; or when I did not love the men, my love was the greater to their books. I had read them and lived with them ; for months they were continually in my thoughts. I seemed to rejoice in their joys and to sorrow with them in their griefs ; and behold, when I came to write of them, my tone was sometimes hardly courteous, and seldom wholly just.' This admission, made with so sympathetic a vibration of the voice, and marked by that frank and manly candour which is one of the writer's most engaging qualities, I must take leave to echo. Every one who essays, in however humble and casual a way, this delicate business of literary criticism, and whose instinct compels him to sift and discriminate, must often be struck by the lack of cordiality which he shows when he comes to put upon paper his impressions of an author who has appealed to him strongly on one side or other of his nature. When he reviews his own judgment, he cannot but be sensible of the hard and unsympathetic nature of his medium. He sees beauties which he might have praised more warmly ; he thinks of blemishes which he might have passed by without censure ; the fear besets him that after all he has succeeded in presenting only an imperfect and distorted idea of the impression which his subject has made upon his own mind. In criticising Mr. Swinburne, I have tried indeed in some measure to reveal his beauties, but I have not sought to cover or minimise his faults. Lest the obligation thus laid upon me should make any one think that I value his fine gifts less highly than I do, that I am not duly grateful for the rich treasures of golden speech with which he has enriched the memories of our race, let me close upon a note of more cordial and whole-hearted admiration; let me say with all earnestness and emphasis that his faults, flagrant as in themselves they are, seem to me slight and trivial when set against the splendour of his merits.

ROBERT FERGUSSON[1]

IN some respects the undisguised and altogether
undisputed pre-eminence of Burns and Scott
among the poets of our own country has not
been without its evil effects.   Shakespeare so
far transcended the other dramatists of his time
that when we speak of the Elizabethan age, in
reference to literature, we think at once of that
great name, and hardly of any one else—hardly
at all of those other dramatists, some of whom
would have furnished forth a lesser time very
creditably.   Just in the same way the very names
of our minor Scots poets are well-nigh forgotten
in the fame of that great pair, Burns and Scott.
This is quite natural, of course ; it is natural that
we should not greatly care to dawdle over *The
Castle of Indolence* or *The Gentle Shepherd*, when
we might be reading or re-reading *Tam o' Shanter*,
or *The Lay of the Last Minstrel*.   But, although
it is natural, one cannot help regretting the comparative neglect into which Thomson and Ramsay

<hr>

[1] *Scots Magazine*, November 1892.

are falling even here in Scotland. As for the poet who is the subject of this paper, Englishmen never knew much of Fergusson, and it is to be feared that most of the generation of Scotsmen which is now growing up are likely through sheer ignorance to take small account of the very special claims which this poor lad possesses on their respect and gratitude. For undoubtedly there are special reasons why Fergusson should keep a warm corner in Scottish hearts which do not apply with equal or nearly equal strength to the cases of Thomson and Ramsay. Thomson was one of those Scotsmen for whom the highroad to London has an irresistible attraction, and when he went away he remained away; in his manner and choice of subjects he is perhaps the least national, the least Scottish of all our poets. Again, one may cherish a hearty feeling of admiration for 'honest Allan,' and yet hold oneself free to confess, as regards his most important work, that though his Shepherd be Gentle, yet, unlike the river Thames, is he also dull.

The case is different with Fergusson. His poetry is worth remembering for its own sake, but a peculiar regard attaches to his name because of the strong influence he had over Burns. The extent of that influence may be at once realised by any one who takes the trouble to compare Fergusson's *Farmer's Ingle* with *The Cottar's Saturday Night* and Fergusson's poem entitled *Leith Races* with *The Holy Fair* of Burns. Burns himself, with that large and generous humanity which makes us so willing to forget or condone his faults, was ever foremost to acknowledge his debt to Fergusson. As is well known, he eagerly sought out, when he came to Edinburgh, Fergusson's unmarked grave in the Canongate churchyard, and, poor and struggling as he then was, put up at his own cost a monument [1] over the remains of the unhappy young man, whom he described, no less truly than pathetically, as his 'elder brother in misfortune.' But notwithstanding the generous praise of his great successor, Fergusson has so strangely been allowed to slip out of sight, that it is only by patient search at the second-hand bookstalls that one can hope to pick up a copy of the poems which once stirred Scotsmen from one end of the kingdom to the other. One can only wonder that a good and adequate edition of Fergusson's works has yet to appear, and surely no very long

---

[1] The following is the inscription, written by Burns, on the stone in the Canongate Churchyard :—

 'No sculptur'd marble here, nor pompous lay,
  No storied urn nor animated bust,
 This simple stone directs pale Scotia's way
  To pour her sorrows o'er her poet's dust.'

time should now be allowed to pass before such an edition is presented to the public. Meanwhile, the aim of this essay is to tell shortly and simply the little there is to tell regarding Fergusson's life, and to say something also of those qualities which have given him the high place he holds among our national poets. To those who know little of Fergusson such an attempt may be welcome; those who already know all that the writer has to tell them may not object to travel in company with him over what, if it is a familiar road, is so because it is also a favourite one.

Robert Fergusson, then, was born in Edinburgh on the 5th of September 1750, in a small house 'whose site is now, it is believed, occupied by North Bridge Street.' Like most of our Scots poets, he was sprung of poor parents. His father, William Fergusson, a native of Tarland in Aberdeenshire, had settled in the metropolis four years before the birth of our poet. Here he could not be said to have fallen on his feet. True, he had found employment, but the sum he received in return for his services was barely sufficient to keep body and soul together, and for many years he was constantly changing his situation, never very greatly for the better. At last, in 1763, thirteen years after the birth of

Robert, he obtained a fairly good appointment as clerk or accountant in the linen department of the British Linen Company; and there he remained till his death.

By all accounts William Fergusson was one of those honest, upright, hard-pushed men, of a type happily familiar enough in Scotland, who have much to suffer at Fortune's hands, but bear up bravely and uncomplainingly through it all. We learn further that he was not without intellectual interests, and even that he had some smack of culture. He took an interest in what his bairns were doing with their Ovid and Horace; those of his letters which have been preserved and printed[1] are not at all badly expressed, and one or two are lit up by a gentle sense of humour. It is said that he, too, had once dallied with the Muse, but any poetical tastes he may have had the stern business of life must have given him very little leisure to indulge. On the whole, one can gather that he was a kind and careful parent, not at all of an austere or illiberal cast of mind; and one naturally thinks with a sigh that had he only lived long enough he would have been able to sympathise with his son's peculiar genius, while at the same time he might have done much to

---

[1] In Mr. A. B. Grosart's valuable edition of 1851, to which my indebtedness is great, and is here very gladly acknowledged.

help the poet to guide his course better than, unfortunately, the poor lad actually did when left to himself. Robert's mother is described as a woman of great worth and piety.

The silent struggles of Scots parents, however poor they may be, to give their children a good schooling, have many times been commented on, and indeed they are often heroic. Robert's father shared the feeling of his class; even when his income was something under £20 a year, he contrived—how he managed it one is at a loss to guess—to spare £1, 15s. for 'school payments.' Robert's education was consequently well cared for. After six months spent with a Mr. Philp, a teacher in Niddry's Wynd, to whom he went at six years of age, he was thought fit for the High School, to which accordingly he was transferred. His progress under all his teachers was rapid, despite his delicate health and the irregularity of attendance which this caused. He early grew to love books, and especially he delighted to study the Bible. When boys come to read the Bible, they generally pick out as their favourite passages those which describe how the children of Israel smote the Amalekites with great slaughter, and such like, but Fergusson seems to have preferred the didactic to the war-like portions. Nor was he content with being a

hearer of the Word; he wished to be a doer—
and a sufferer—also, and if others failed in their
obvious duty, it lay upon him to point this out.
So, after poring over the Proverbs of Solomon, he
astonished his mother by asking her to give him
a whipping. The good woman asked the reason
of so novel a request. 'Oh, mother,' replied the
precocious youth, '"He that spareth the rod
spoileth the child."'

At the High School Fergusson remained four
years. At the end of that time he obtained,
through the influence of Lord Findlater, a bursary,
which took him first to the Grammar-School of
Dundee, and afterwards to the University of
St. Andrews. He entered the University in the
fifteenth year of his age, and soon began to single
himself out as a youth of ready wit and genial
temper. Curiously enough, mathematics, rather
than the classics, took his fancy. Virgil and
Horace, he said, were the only classical authors
he cared to look at. The tedium of his studies
he relieved by playing pranks and stringing
rhymes. He wrote satires on the professors;
gentle and genial enough in all probability, for
Fergusson's satire amused, but never stung or
festered. It is said that while at the University
he was at work on a more serious effort—a tragedy,
namely, on the life of Sir William Wallace; and

the story is probable enough, for the two eternally
fascinating subjects which suggest themselves to
Scotsmen with generous minds and a turn for
rhyming are Sir William Wallace and Mary,
Queen of Scots.   But poetry was only one outlet
for his high spirits, and Fergusson once or twice
got into rather laughable scrapes.   There is no
need, however, to magnify these as some of his
biographers have done.   The most serious of
them was a college row, for his share in which he
was formally 'extruded.' But even in this case the
offence was evidently not very serious, for he was
received back in a day or two.   An amusing and
characteristic story is told of another of these
playful pranks.   Fergusson had a very fine voice,
and in consequence was often selected to act as
precentor.   He did not greatly care for this post
of dignity, and he resolved to get rid of it.   So
one day he asked the congregation (no doubt in a
voice sepulchrally solemn), as if reading from a
'line' which had been handed in, 'to remember
in prayer a young man (then present) of whom,
from the sudden effects of inebriety, there appears
but small hope of recovery.'   He was not asked
to act as precentor again.

Fergusson had originally been intended for the
ministry ; but the untimely death of his father,
who died during his college course, leaving the

widow in very poor circumstances, forced Robert
to give up all thought of a profession for which
he was not, in truth, too well fitted. Even in
those days, when the dignity and decorous dulness of the pulpit were not so jealously guarded
as they are now, a few freaks such as that which
relieved him of the office of precentor might not
improbably have brought his pastoral career to as
sudden a close ; and, on the whole, it is perhaps
as well that the risk was not run. Fergusson
had never looked with much favour on the pro-
posal to clap a black coat on his back ; still, it
cannot have been with very pleasant feelings that
he found himself, after four years' study at the
University, flung on the world, and under the
necessity of doing something at once to help his
mother to maintain their humble household. He
had a maternal uncle in Aberdeenshire who was
in fairly prosperous circumstances, and to his
house Fergusson went for a time. But an unlucky
incident, which has been most unduly magnified,
and into the particulars of which it is not necessary to enter here, destroyed any hopes he may
have had of substantial aid from that quarter, and
on his return to his well-loved Edinburgh Fergusson looked out for something to which he might
turn his hand. He was not long in obtaining a
poor employment as a copyist of legal papers in

the Commissary-Clerk's office. There, with the exception of a few months spent in the Sheriff-Clerk's office, Fergusson passed the remaining years of his life. The work was a routine of the most mechanical character, and the pittance Fergusson received was of the poorest. The 'daily drudgery at the desk's dead wood,' as Charles Lamb phrased it, did not suit Fergusson; and besides, a close view of its working does not seem to have bred in him any great liking for the law. In one stanza he condenses the experience of, it is to be feared, many thousand unfortunate litigants :—

> ' But law's a draw-well—unco deep,
> Withouten rim fouk out to keep ;
> A donnart chiel, when drunk, may dreep
> Fu' sleely in,
> But finds the gait baith stey an' steep
> Ere out he win.'

But Fergusson, despite the prosaic character of his occupation, did not long allow his poetical talents to lie fallow. In 1771 he began to contribute to Ruddiman's *Weekly Magazine*, then a well-known Edinburgh journal, the poems on which his fame depends. He did not, however, find his true level at the outset. His first poems were in English, and the praise injudiciously bestowed upon these led him to continue for a while to write in a language in which it is evident he could never have achieved anything worth remembering. But a poet may generally be trusted to discover sooner or later in what direction his strength really lies, and it was not long before Fergusson started that vein of Scots dialect in which he was to work with rich results. The public, too, were quick to note the difference: Fergusson's fame began to penetrate to village after village, and the weekly instalment of the magazine came to be looked forward to with a new and eager interest, not in the metropolis only, but all over Scotland.

Unfortunately, while his fame was steadily growing, Fergusson was leading a life which one cannot contemplate with any degree of pleasure. His home was a poor one, his work was monotonous, and the social bent of his temper inclined him to make up for his daily slavery by unchecked conviviality when his work was done. He takes a peculiar delight in describing his potations: ' he recalls,' to quote Mr. R. L. Stevenson, who has written admirably of Fergusson, ' he recalls a supper-party pleasantry with something akin to tenderness ; and sounds the praises of the act of drinking as if it were virtuous, or, at least, witty in itself. It was not choice,' he adds, ' so much as external fate, that kept Fergusson in this round of sordid pleasures. A Scot of poetic temperament, and without religious exaltation, drops, as if by nature, into the public-house.' And then Mr. Stevenson has a characteristic fling at the atrocious climate which has banished him to Samoa. 'The picture,' he says, 'may not be a pleasant one, but what is a man to do in this dog's weather.' This may seem to some a rather fatalistic doctrine, but surely every one will agree in the force of the plea that Fergusson deserves pity rather than blame. Life in Edinburgh at that time had nothing very pleasing or attractive for those of his class and circumstances except the public-house parlour; one has only to turn to his poems to see that. 'O sir!' said Fergusson to one who remonstrated seriously with him, 'anything to forget my poor mother and these aching fingers.'

With this new-born love of dissipation he was as fond as ever of practical joking. One evening in a frolic he laid a wager that he would sell a bundle of ballads. Accordingly he disguised himself, took the ballads in his hand, and sang Scots songs so sweetly, that a crowd soon gathered round him. In a few moments he sold off his whole stock, and returned laughing to his companions, to spend the proceeds in conviviality.

The end soon drew near. His irregular habits weakened a constitution never robust: a cold, caught during the stirring scenes of an election,

such as he has described in one of the most
spirited and broadly humorous of his poems, had
disastrous results. He fell into complete religious
despondency, and was soon on the verge of madness. Once, however, he rallied, and was beginning to be more himself, but just at this time a
fall from a staircase brought on an acute mania
which made necessary his removal to the old
Darien House, then the only public asylum in
Edinburgh. It is said that just as he was entering
the gates of this dismal mansion a glimpse of consciousness visited him; realising where he was being
taken to, he uttered a piercing shriek, which was
echoed by the unhappy inmates, and lingered long
in the ears of the relatives who accompanied him.

Fergusson's time was not long in this house of
misery. Restless at first, thinking himself a king,
and plaiting a crown of straw to place upon his
head, he afterwards quieted down, and was quite
peaceable when his mother and sister came to see
him. 'He thanked them for their kindness, and
asked his sister to bring her seam and sit beside
him.' There was even talk of his release; but
two months passed away, and Fergusson still
hovered in the mental twilight between lunacy
and sanity. When at last the release came, it was
to be other than they dreamed of. His mother
and sister were constant in their kindness. Of one

interview, which was to be their last, a peculiarly affecting account has been preserved. 'The evening was chilly and damp. His feet felt very cold. He asked his mother to gather up the bed-clothes and sit upon them. She did so. He looked wistfully at her, and said, "O mother, this is kind indeed!" But again he complained that his feet were "cold, cold." When they prepared to leave, he entreated them to remain. "Do not go, mother, yet; do not leave me." It was the time, however, for "shutting up." They parted.' Before the morning came Robert Fergusson's short life was spent. He died on the 16th of October 1774.

If anything could add to the regret at so untimely a death, it would be the fact that his prospects seemed brighter now than they had ever been. A collected edition of the poems contributed to Ruddiman's Magazine had been published in 1773. The book had sold rapidly, and Fergusson's fame might now be looked upon as secure. Nor was this all. His brother Henry, who had been a rather wild youth, and who had betaken himself to the sea, like so many more wild youths before and since, had sent home a remittance, and Fergusson's home was in process of being brightened up. Another generous deed, of which no record of Fergusson should omit to take account, falls also to be mentioned here. A

gentleman named Burnet, who had been one of
Fergusson's friends, had gone out to India, and
prospered there.   With a generosity which directly does himself infinite credit, and which indirectly bears testimony to Fergusson's worth (for
such a friendship must have been based upon a
very real regard), he sent home a cordial invitation to Fergusson to join him in India, accom-
panying the offer with a remittance of £100 to
pay expenses.   But this munificence came too
late.   Before the letter reached Edinburgh Fergusson had already been laid in the grave.   One
is pleased to add that the money was handed
over to Fergusson's family, to make of it what use
they pleased.

Such is the story of Fergusson's life—short and
wretched enough in all conscience, shorter and
more wretched even than that of Burns.   He
seems to have been a kindly, genial soul, generous
in feeling, full of fun, fond of practical joking, and
with no worse faults than a certain weakness of
character and that unlucky devotion to Bacchus.
' He was,' said the porter at the St. Andrews
University,—' He was a tricky callant, but a fine
laddie for a' that.'   And the homely sentence
sums up Fergusson's character with absolute
precision and fitness.

In our estimate of Fergusson's poetry his

English pieces do not count. 'These English songs,' said Burns, 'gravel me to death,' and it is easy to imagine Fergusson saying the same thing.

> ' No choiring warblers flutter in the sky ;
>   Phœbus no longer holds his radiant sway ;
>   While Nature, with a melancholy eye,
>   Bemoans the loss of his departed ray.'

That is a measure of Fergusson's English performance ; and for most people it will be quite enough. Clearly, had Fergusson written always in this fashion, one would not be talking of him at this time of day. Indeed, if there is one thing more than another specially noticeable in Fergusson, it is the rich feast of the Doric which in every one of his best poems he sets before us. Such phrases as 'gust your gab' and 'weet your thrapple' ought to be dear to the heart of every patriotic Scot, and of such phrases Fergusson is full. Not Burns himself has a greater command over the resources of our kindly Scots tongue. If we valued our poets in proportion to the difficulty which the base Southron finds in reading their works, then would Fergusson be elevated far above Burns. Without going quite so far as that, one has a certain malicious satisfaction in trying to guess what one who has the misfortune not to be a Scotsman would make of this address *To the Tron-Kirk Bell* :—

> 'Wanwordy, crazy, dinsome thing,
>   As e'er was framed to jow or ring !
> What gar'd them sic in steeple hing,
>   They ken themsel ;
> But weel wat I, they couldna bring
>   Waur sounds frae hell.
>
> .   .   .   .   .   .
>
> 'Oh ! were I provost o' the toun,
> I swear by a' the powers aboon,
> I 'd bring ye wi' a reesle doun ;
>   Nor should ye think
> (Sae sair I 'd crack an' clour your crown)
>   Again to clink.
>
> .   .   .   .   .
>
> 'But, far frae thee the bailies dwell,
> Or they would scunner at your knell ;
> Gie the foul thief his riven bell,
>   And then, I trow,
> The byword hauds, " The deil himsel
>   Has got his due." '
>
> .   .   .   .   .

This familiar way of treating the august personage referred to is, I think, very characteristic of our Scots poets. And the reason seems clear. It is not hard to hate the Devil, but, in spite of yourself, you cannot but have a friendly, neighbourly sort of feeling for one whom you call, familiarly, the Deil.

Fergusson has been called the Laureate of Old Edinburgh, and the title is richly deserved.

There he had been born, there he spent most of
his life, and he came, as most do, to love the old
grey city right well.   With his quick eye and his
true descriptive power he contrives to give us, in
a wonderfully vivid fashion, an idea of what life
in the chief of Scottish cities was like in the last
years of the eighteenth century. *Auld Reekie,
The Daft Days, The King's Birthday, The Election,
Caller Oysters, Leith Races*—how picturesquely
these bring before us the old, quaint town, with
all the bustle and humours of the streets, the dirt,
the smells, the merry din of the change-houses,
and the drunkenness, the cheerful, the deliberate
drunkenness, of its douce citizens.

Here, then, lay Fergusson's strength, in describing in his quietly humorous and satirical
fashion the city scenes he knew so well, and had
joined in so often.   He was not without a feeling
for Nature, of course—witness the idyllic close of
that rollicking poem, *The King's Birthday,*—but
he had been born among the high lands of Edinburgh, and it was of Edinburgh that he wrote
best.   Dealing with such themes as the street
scenes suggested, his verse naturally lacked
dignity and elevation, but at least—and this was
much—it was true to life; he described only
what he saw, always he wrote 'with his eye on
the object.'

Fergusson had neither the fire nor the pathos of
Burns; love had not come to him as it came
to Burns, causing spontaneous bursts of song.
His experience was not mature; seriousness, that
deep and true view of life which only the progress
of the years can bring, was wanting; dying at
twenty-four, how could it have been otherwise?
But through all his best poems there runs a tone
of genuine humour and sarcasm, always pleasant
and sometimes pungent. Thus he sings satirically
the praises of *Gude Braid Claith* :—

> ' Braid claith lends fouk an unco heeze ;
>   Maks mony kail-worms butterflees ;
>   Gies mony a doctor his degrees,
>   For little skaith :
>   In short, you may be what you please,
>   Wi' gude braid claith.
>
> .   .   .   .   .
>
> ' For tho' ye had as wise a snout on,
>   As Shakespeare or Sir Isaac Newton,
>   Your judgment fouk wad hae a doubt on,
>   I 'll tak my aith,
>   Till they could see ye wi' a suit on
>   O' gude braid claith.'

Let me conclude my quotations with one which
shows how sweet a strain Fergusson was master of
once in a while. It occurs in the *Elegy on the
Death of Scots Music.* He complains, a hundred
years before Professor Blackie, of the neglect of
our national airs, and asks—

> 'Could lavrocks, at the dawnin' day,
>   Could linties, chirmin' frae the spray,
>   Or todlin' burns, that smoothly play
>   Owre gowden bed,
>   Compare wi' "Birks o' Invermay"?
>   But now they're dead.'

What Fergusson might have achieved had he lived it is idle to speculate. He died, insane, at twenty-four; but already his work was done. In his habit of dealing directly with the subjects that lay nearest to his hand—dealing with them faithfully and freely in the homely tongue he so well knew how to use,—in this habit he had shown the way to Burns, he had marked out the path which he who had the good fortune to come after was to tread with a firmer, a more assured step. He is thus linked with that great movement in English poetry of which Wordsworth was—not so much the originator as—the first wholly conscious exponent. When we talk of Wordsworth as having reformed English poetry by freeing it from the bonds of artifice, by informing it with a greater depth of thought, and by achieving a new and admirable simplicity of style and diction, we talk with a certain degree of looseness. He was not the first in this great work; before him there was Cowper and there was Burns, to name no more than these. Cowper had right ideas; but

his work, admirable as in many respects it is, had
not sufficient weight to stand against the work of
masters like Dryden and Pope, whose methods
he rightly enough condemned. The best work of
Burns, again, one might almost say his only good
work, was done in poems which, from the fact of
their being written in the Scots tongue, were in
great part unintelligible to English readers. The
moment Burns came to write in English he
became a slave to artifice, he declined into a
diction altogether infelicitous, sometimes even
barbarous. More than that, Burns was not a
conscious reformer : he worked for the new ideas,
but unconsciously, at least not of set purpose.
But by his Scottish poems he exerted an influence
on Wordsworth the extent of which that magnanimous egotist was not slow to acknowledge.
Every one will remember Wordsworth's fine
tribute to the memory of the poet :—

> 'Whose light I hailed when first it shone,
> When, breaking forth as Nature's own,
>   It showed my youth
> How verse may build a princely throne
>   On humble truth.'

And what we have now to remember is that
the influence thus described was passed on from
Ramsay to Fergusson, from Fergusson to Burns.
Fergusson especially it was who inspired and

stimulated the early efforts of Burns. 'Meeting with Fergusson's Scottish Poems, I strung anew my wildly-sounding lyre with emulating vigour': that is what Burns himself says, and surely it should of itself suffice to keep Fergusson's memory alive among us. That his poems served to set and keep Burns on the right path remains, after all is said, Fergusson's best and highest claim on our consideration; but surely it is no slight one!

THE POETRY AND OTHER WRITINGS
OF JAMES RUSSELL LOWELL[1]

> ' Primores populi arripuit populumque tributim,
>   Scilicet uni aequus virtuti atque ejus amicis.'
>
> HOR. *Sat.* ii. 1.

THERE are few great names in American literature ; compared with the rich harvests of
imaginative work which our own and other
European countries have reaped and stored during
centuries of placid existence, the great Western
Republic can point only to a few scanty ears of
corn, garnered but yesterday, as it seems, and with
the dew yet fresh upon them.

It is in the nature of things that this should be
so, for, as the lives of nations go, America is
hardly yet out of her 'teens. Nor have the
peculiar circumstances of her history been favourable to the growth of literature and the arts.
Her first settlers were austere Puritans, and these
'stern men with empires in their brains' looked
upon the Fine Arts with mingled contempt and
hatred, as so many devices of the devil with

---

[1] Written 1894. Hitherto unpublished.

which he snared the souls of men.   The struggle for bare subsistence was hardly over when the infant country was called to a death-grapple with her kinsmen across the seas.   The triumphant close of that struggle, again, was coincident with the beginning of the modern commercial era, and America lay for long bound in the iron grip of the commercial spirit, straining every nerve to get rich, wholly absorbed, it might have seemed, by the stress and strain and turmoil of the modern world. But a spiritual flowering-time was at hand, and New England, about the middle of the present century, experienced what we might almost call a literary ' revival.'

Mr. James Russell Lowell was one of the most brilliant and versatile of that gifted band who have effectually redeemed American literature from the charge of barrenness, and charmed the readers of two hemispheres.   It is too soon yet to attempt to decide what place Mr. Lowell will ultimately be accorded in the literary hierarchy which includes such men as Emerson, Hawthorne, Longfellow, Holmes, and Whittier, but certainly it must be a high one.   In mere exquisiteness of workmanship Hawthorne certainly surpasses him, and his influence on the thought of the time was not so profound, suggestive, and stimulating as that of Emerson.   But he was perhaps the best all-round man of letters whom America has yet produced. Other writers may excel him in one thing or another, but no one has turned his talents to such good purpose in so many different fields of literary labour. He wrote for fully half a century ; in turn he was serious poet, satirical verse-maker, literary critic, political controversialist, and essayist on all sorts of out-of-the-way subjects. And nearly every page he wrote is worth reading, for all his work is marked—not only by high literary excellence, but—by a brilliance and verve, a robust faith in himself, his own opinions, and his own country, that are exhilarating and delightful. With the solitary exception of Walt Whitman, he seems to me the most distinctively national of American men of letters of the highest rank ; his works are racier of the soil than either the delicate, sensitive, and shrinking genius of Hawthorne or the transcendentalism of Emerson. Mr. Lowell, however, was national in no petty or exclusive sense, and to all who 'speak the tongue which Shakespeare spake' his death was a loss keenly felt and honestly deplored. To this country, indeed, Mr. Lowell was bound by peculiar ties, and we felt that we also had a share in his triumphs. As Ambassador to the Court of St. James, he represented what was highest and best in American society, and we for our part felt that we were honoured by his presence among us, that we honoured ourselves by paying him the highest honours in our power to confer and in his will to accept. No literary man could propose to himself a nobler task than that of binding together the two great branches of the Anglo-Saxon race, and during the later years of his life Mr. Lowell did more towards that end than even Mr. Carnegie, with his almost incredible want of tact and taste, can undo.

It is pleasant to think that as time laid its mellowing hand upon him his old asperity towards England died away, and that he loved us more as he came to know us better. And so it came about that when 'Trade's new Mercury' with her 'flame-winged feet' carried the news of his death over two continents, our own country and his native land alike felt that in him they had lost a common friend, and the two great nations clasped hands beside the grave of one who had been very helpful and very dear to both.

To most people both here and in America Mr. Lowell is best known as the author of the *Biglow Papers*; as the man, that is, who brought back what almost seemed the lost art of satire. He was long in gaining the public ear with his serious verse, but from the first the *Biglow Papers* went like wild-fire. The success was thoroughly deserved ; it is not too much to say that this admirable work effaces everything that has been done for a long time in this department; since Byron's *English Bards and Scotch Reviewers* nothing in satiric verse can for a moment be set beside this veritable *tour de force.* In truth, Mr Lowell had all the qualifications for his task ; he knew his countrymen well, he had a keen eye for character, a wit at once caustic and genial, and a happy turn for homely and striking images. In facility of rhyme he rivals Butler ; as a master of the gentle art of punning he outdistances Hood. And behind, and animating these, were his thoroughgoing belief in the righteousness of his cause, his deep and heart-felt desire for the moral regeneration of his fellow-citizens, his honest hatred for everything mean, base, and cowardly. 'American humour' is responsible for some strange and monstrous births, but here we have the genuine smack of the soil, and every one who reads Mr. Lowell must remember him with gratitude as one who did much to lighten up this dull world of ours with laughter. Hosea Biglow, and Birdofreedum Sawin, and the Rev. Homer Wilbur—that most delightful of pedants —who that has read the book can forget these ? They dwell in our memory with our favourite characters in fiction ; for indeed they are all *creations*, so genuine, so life-like, that one can only wonder why Mr. Lowell, who tried so much else, did not also turn his hand to fiction. May I confess an especial fondness for the old clergyman? With his amusing garrulity, his strange mixture of pedantry and practical good sense, of Yankee shrewdness and child-like simplicity, of ponderous solemnity and sly, half-unconscious humour, he seems to me worthy of a place alongside the elder Shandy of Laurence Sterne. Let no one in his haste, or in the vain imagination of his heart, or in terror at the profusion of Latin quotations, skip the reverend gentleman's prose introductions to the poems, for they are as delightful and as inimitable in their way as the poems themselves. Nor should one omit to read among the *Notices of an Independent Press* the extract from *The World-Harmonic-Æolian-attachment*—that delightful and good-humoured travesty of Carlyle, with just the requisite touch of caricature and no more.

The *Biglow Papers* were published in two series, the first condemning the war with Mexico into which the United States entered in 1846, the second advocating the side of the North in the great Civil War. The subjects, then, are not such as would of themselves be expected to interest us greatly ; but so strong and so excellent is Mr.

Lowell's handling, that they do interest us, and interest us profoundly. They throw a strong light on some of the meaner aspects of public life in America, and they abound in humorous reflections on the little ways of politicians which every one can enjoy.

We have all heard of the gentleman who opines that

> 'A marciful Providence fashioned us holler
>   In order that we might our principles swaller.'

And we all know, or imagine we know, the sort of candidate who might, in a moment of unwonted frankness, unbosom himself thus :—

> 'I 'm an eclectic ; ez to choosin'
>   'Twixt this an' thet, I 'm plaguy lawth ;
> I leave a side thet looks like losin',
>   But (wile there 's doubt) I stick to both.
>
> .   .   .   .   .   .
>
> Ez to my principles, I glory
>   In hevin' nothin' o' the sort ;
> I ain't a Wig, I ain't a Tory,
>   I 'm jest a *candidate*, in short.'

Gentlemen who have to undergo that pleasing process known to the initiated as a Scottish heckling might do worse than take a lesson from the very frank and lucid manner in which this amiable eclectic explains his views on the Slavery question :—

> 'Ez to the slaves, there's no confusion
>   In *my* idees consarnin' them,—
> *I* think they air an Institution,
>   A sort of—yes, jest so,—ahem ;
> Do *I* own any? Of my merit
>   On thet pint yourself may jedge ;
> All is, I never drink no sperit,
>   Nor I hain't never signed no pledge.'

Again, how well the tendency to rest the claims of public men on anything rather than the principles they do, or do not, possess, how well this tendency is made fun of in one of Mr. Sawin's epistles!—

> 'Ef while you're 'lectioneering round some curus chaps should beg
> To know my views of State affairs, jest answer *Wooden Leg.*
> Ef they ain't satisfied with that, and kin' o' pry and doubt
> And ax for somethin' definit', jest say *One Eye Put Out.*
> Thet kind o' talk, I guess, you'll find 'll answer like a charm,
> And when you're drew tu nigh the wall, hold up my missin' arm.
> Ef they should nose roun' for a pledge, put on a vartoous look,
> An' tell 'em thet's precisely what I never giv'—nor took.
> Then you can call me Timbertoes—thet's wut the people likes,
> Somethin' combinin' morril truth with phrases sech as strikes.
> Old Timbertoes, ye see, 's a creed it's safe to be quite bold on,
> There's nothin' in 't the other side can anyways get hold on.'

But it would be to give a wrong idea of the *Biglow Papers* if we alluded only to the pungency

of its wit and sarcasm. *The Courtin'* is a delight-
fully humorous idyll of country lovemaking, and
other pieces of the series rise into a loftier sphere
than that of pungent comment on the corruption
and self-seeking of Southern politicians. If a
keen sense of humour is an excellent corrective
of extravagance, it often acts as an effectual
damper on enthusiasm ; the humorist has usually
a dread of waxing enthusiastic over anything, lest
fools should call him mad. The Puritan strain
in Mr. Lowell's blood would seem to have saved
him from becoming a cynic or a humorist merely.
The fine apostrophe beginning ' O strange New
World, that yet wast never young ' is so well
known that quotation were an impertinence.
When we remember that Lowell lost two nephews
in the war, the pathos of Hosea's lament goes
straight to the heart :—

> ' Why, hain't I held 'em on my knee ?
>   Didn't I love to see 'em growin',
> Three likely lads ez wal could be,
>   Hahnsome and brave, an' not tu knowin' ?
> I set and look into the blaze,
>   Whose nature, jest like theirn, keeps climbin'
> Ez long 'z it lives, in shinin' ways,
>   *An' half despise myself for rhymin'.* '

And the longing for ' Peace with Honour ' must
have found an echo in thousands of hearts towards
the close of that long and bitter struggle, the very

memory of which is now happily fading into the
past :—

> ' Come, Peace ! not like a mourner bowed
>   For honour lost an' dear ones wasted,
> But proud, to meet a people proud,
>   With eyes that tell o' triumph tasted !
> Come, with han' grippin' on the hilt,
>   An' step that proves ye Victory's daughter !
> Longin' for you, our sperits wilt
>   Like shipwrecked men's on raf's for water ! '

Here, as elsewhere, Mr. Lowell proves, as Burns
did before him, as Mr. Kipling is doing even now,
how much may be done by a man of genius with
a dialect seemingly so uncouth as to be unfitted
for the higher purposes of poetry.

The *Fable for Critics*, its author tells us, was a
mere *jeu d'esprit*, extemporised for his own amuse-
ment, and with no thought of publication.   Edgar
Allan Poe, that unhappy literary Ishmael, whose
hand was against every man, loudly proclaimed
that by its publication Mr. Lowell had committed
an irrevocable *faux pas*, and lowered himself at
least fifty per cent. in literary public opinion.[1]

---

[1] The ' three-fifths sheer genius and two-fifths sheer fudge' had
evidently rankled.   Poe's articles (vol. iv. of his *Collected Works*)
rank among the curiosities of criticism.   His tone is curiously,
even intensely, provincial ; he is capable of humour of this schoolboy sort : ' Mr. M. is execrable, but Mr. C. is $(x+1)$ execrable' ;
and many articles deal with names now altogether forgotten.   But
he had flashes of insight, and there are some passages finely
phrased and of remarkable discrimination.

We must agree with him in condemning the
rambling and incoherent plot, and the monotonous jingle of the versification; but the estimates
of American authors are brilliantly executed, and,
on the whole, remarkably fair and just. To call
it a great poem would be absurd, but it is
certainly as brilliant a piece of doggerel as ever
was written, and the riot of puns would bring a
smile to the face of the least risible of mortals.

I have chosen to begin my study of Mr.
Lowell's works with a review of his satirical and
humorous verse, because it is as a satirist and
humorist that Mr. Lowell is best known. And
indeed, I cannot think that those are wise friends
of Mr. Lowell who seek to put the *Biglow Papers*
out of sight because they draw attention away
from his serious poetry. They protest too much.
To have written the best political satire since
Absalom and Achitophel is after all no mean
achievement. At the same time I should be
willing to admit that Mr. Lowell's more ambitious
work has not, especially on this side of the
Atlantic, received the attention which it deserves.
Not that it can be claimed for Mr. Lowell that he
is one of the few supreme masters of the art of
poetry; his place is not with Shakespeare or
Milton, hardly even with Dryden or Shelley or
Keats. He lacks, somehow, the supreme and

indefinable charm of these great masters.   Indeed
I cannot help thinking that Hawthorne, although
he wrote in prose, had more of the poet in him,
more of the poet's instinctive sense of the magical
charm which lies in words, more of the poet's
unfailing felicity in evoking that charm, than
most, if not all, of his poetical brethren.
'Brilliant' is perhaps the word that characterises
best Mr. Lowell's work, alike in poetry and in
prose, and surely brilliant is *not* the word that
rises to our lips as we think of a scene from
Shakespeare, a sonnet of Wordsworth, or a stanza
of Keats.   One feels, too, that Mr. Lowell's
brilliance sometimes degenerates into what, if I
must speak plainly, I should call a vicious smart-
ness, and genius is rarely smart.

It may be as well to give an example of what
I mean.   In his excellent study of Dryden, Mr.
Lowell takes Dryden to task, justly, for the line

'Heaven would no bargain for its blessings drive.'

In one of his finest poems—*The Cathedral*—the
following passage occurs :—

'Doubtless his church will be no hospital
  For superannuate forms and mumping shams,
  No parlour where men *issue policies*
  Of life-assurance on the Eternal Mind.'

He would be a bold critic who should say that
Dryden's line is more objectionable than this.

There is too much of this sort of thing in Mr. Lowell's poetry, and it is surely unsatisfactory.

It would almost seem as though Mr. Lowell's fluency, his superabundance of wit, often led him to say things that his cooler critical judgment would condemn as out of place in poetry. Professor Nichol's criticism, that 'Mr. Lowell has on most occasions "enough of wit," but seldom "as much again to govern it,"' would seem to be fully justified. He had not the haunting passion of the artist for absolute perfection of form, nor the restraint and rigorous self-judgment which go so far towards the production of perfect artistic work. Lovers of the classics may perhaps think that it was this spirit which made him prefer to Greek sculpture, with its stern and bare simplicity, its pure and straight lines, the grandiose irregularities and the occasional grotesqueness of Gothic architecture.[1] For music of the rarer and haunting sort he is too prone to offer as a substitute rhetoric, doubtless of a very stirring kind, but which must be ranked on a lower plane than true poetry, which of all things is most removed from rhetoric. In Mr. Lowell's most ambitious poems the cloven hoof of the rhetorician too often peeps out beneath the singing robes of the poet.

Arnold draws a very lively picture of some of

[1] See *The Cathedral.*

Wordsworth's most pompous verses being recited before a Social Science Congress. 'One can call up the whole scene. A great room in one of our dismal provincial towns; dusty air and jaded afternoon daylight; benches full of men with bald heads and women with spectacles; an orator lifting up his face from a manuscript to declaim these lines of Wordsworth; and in the soul of any poor child of nature who may have wandered in thither an unutterable sense of lamentation and mourning and woe.'

If for Wordsworth we substitute Lowell, and for Social Science Congress an Anti-Slavery gathering, the passage represents only too truly what we sometimes feel in reading Mr. Lowell.

> 'Not here, O Apollo,
> Are haunts meet for thee.'

The professional critics differ curiously as to the value of Mr. Lowell's more ambitious poems. Thus, Mr. H. D. Traill—a very competent judge, one would think — applies the epithet 'truly splendid' to the great *Commemoration Ode*. On the other hand, hear Mr. Swinburne, who speaks with the authority of a master of the craft. He describes it as 'a thanksgiving ode of wooden verse, sawn into unequal planks, and tagged incongruously with tuneless bells, . . . modelled on the chaotic songs of ceremony done to order on state occasions by our laureates of the Restoration and the Revolution.'   Where doctors differ——? But Mr. Swinburne, as we know, is apt to be 'over-violent or over-civil,' and perhaps the truth lies between the two.   The ode is perhaps the most difficult of all poetical forms, if one may judge from the few unequivocal successes in this sort—a form also in which it would almost seem that there is no half-way house between complete triumph and dire and irremediable failure.   Of Mr. Lowell's Ode it can hardly be said to evolve itself with the sure and orderly progression, for it rather proceeds by fits and starts, and here and there an unlucky word or phrase pulls us to earth again.   But not even Mr. Swinburne himself, plead he never so eloquently, could persuade us that the lines which follow are not fine poetry :—

> 'Before my musing eye
> The mighty ones of old sweep by
> Disvoicëd now and insubstantial things,
> As noisy once as we ; poor ghosts of kings,
> Shadows of empire wholly gone to dust,
> And many races, nameless long ago,
> To darkness driven by that imperious gust
> Of ever-rushing Time that here doth blow ;
> O visionary world, condition strange,
> Where nought abiding is but only Change,
> Where the deep-bolted stars themselves
> Still shift and range !'

Doubtless Mr. Lowell does not always remain at this high level, but the level *is* high, and what would become of most of our poets if we demanded of them that they should always give us of their best—what would become, for example, of Wordsworth, who is so deplorably unequal—what even of Shakespeare himself? The critic must certainly set himself to see what *is* best, and to mark clearly this from what is not so good ; but he is inexcusable if he is so intent on seeing blemishes that he is blinded to the presence of beauties.

I should have liked to dwell at some length on some of Mr. Lowell's longer poems, but the limits assigned to this essay forbid the attempt. I can only refer in passing to the *Vision of Sir Launfal*, with its admirable contrast between June and winter, and its fine moral :—

> ' The Holy Supper is kept, indeed,
> In whatso we share with another's need ;
> Not in what we give but in what we share,
> For the gift without the giver is bare.
> Who gives himself with his alms feeds three,—
> Himself, his hungering neighbour, and me.'

And in particular, I should have liked to analyse *The Cathedral*, which takes the first place among Mr. Lowell's more purely reflective poems. No-where, perhaps, do Mr. Lowell's conservative instincts come out so clearly as here, nowhere has he given such perfect expression to his love of that

> 'beautiful Old Time, now hid away
> In the Past's valley of Avilion.'

In an age when religious doubt is regarded as the hall-mark of intellectual superiority, Mr. Lowell would seem to have preserved unfalteringly the faith of his fathers. He could hardly reconcile himself to

> 'This nineteenth century, with its knife and glass,
> That make thought physical, and thrust far off
> The heaven, so neighbourly with man of old,
> *To voids sparse-sown with alienated stars.*
>
> .   .   .   .   .   .
>
> Science was Faith once ; Faith were Science now,
> Would she but lay her bow and arrows by
> And arm her with the weapons of the time.
> *Nothing that keeps thought out is safe from thought.*

The last line has the pithiness of Pope.   I cannot but think this a beautiful poem—beautiful in thought, and beautiful in expression.

If we sometimes in Mr. Lowell's Odes miss the breath of inspiration, many of his shorter pieces have an inimitable freshness, fragrance, and spontaneity.   The *Voyage to Vinland*, for example, is an admirable specimen of the heroic poem, and such verses as those entitled *Auf Wiederschen*, and the poem beginning

> 'O tell me less or tell me more,
> Soft eyes with mystery at the core,'

are eminently pretty and graceful love-poems. Deeper in feeling, and admirable in art, is the poem *Das Ewig Weibliche*, the first stanza of which I cannot deny myself the pleasure of quoting.

> ' How was I worthy so divine a loss,
>   Deepening my midnights, kindling all my morns?
> Why waste such precious wood to make my cross,
>   Such far-sought roses for my crown of thorns?'

Those who hold the modern formula of ' Art for Art's sake' in its extremest form object to Mr. Lowell's poems that they are overloaded with moralising. If he sinned in this way, it was at all events with his eyes open.[1] His conception of the poet's function was radically different from that held by those who think that his highest aim is merely to please the ear of the literary epicure. For him the poet was no mere

> ' empty rhymer,
> Who lies with idle elbow on the grass,
> And fits his singing, like a cunning timer,
> To all men's prides and fancies as they pass.'

He was rather the prophet and seer, whose duty it was to speak to the highest and noblest in men's natures, to lift them up to a loftier level of life and thought. The ideal is a high one, but Mr. Lowell has left nothing behind him which is

[1] See in the *Fable for Critics* his criticism of himself.

unworthy of it. He was a poet in whose favour Plato might have made an exception from the decree which banished all such from his ideal republic. He must be very insensible to the power and influence of noble poetry who does not rise from the study of Mr. Lowell's works with a sense of having communed with a noble and reverent nature, with a deeper hatred towards sin and vice, and a firmer will to hold by those things which are pure and lovely and of good report. And we may be confident that praise of this sort is what Mr. Lowell would have valued most highly.

Among Mr. Lowell's many claims to the respect and admiration of the reading public, his critical essays rank next, perhaps, to his poetry. The department of criticism is one in which our literature has, so far, been singularly unprolific, as compared, for example, with those of France and Germany. Mr. Lowell must certainly be accorded one of the highest places in that scanty band of our men of letters who have made a business of criticism. He had not, indeed, Matthew Arnold's Olympian air, his engaging suavity of manner, his 'serene felicity of phrase,'[1] his gift of fine irony, all the keener because it is so perfectly courteous. But on the other hand,

[1] W. E. Henley : *Views and Reviews.*

he was free from Arnold's mannerisms and over-fastidiousness, and often he seems to go deeper than the fascinating apostle of 'sweetness and light.' I know hardly any critical essays so fitted as his to inspire a just and sane enthusiasm for the masterpieces of literature. He had in full measure those first and most essential qualities of a critic—a real gusto for good literature, and a real insight into what is fine in literature and what is not so fine. His literary tastes were broad and catholic; he recognised that the House Beautiful of Art has many mansions. For the most part his literary judgments are eminently sane and sensible; he wrote out of the fulness of knowledge, with a rare and cosmopolitan culture, but with scarcely a trace of pedantry. Ripe scholar as he was, he bore his load of learning lightly, and rarely sacrificed to the great and peculiarly British Goddess of Dulness. His spirits were almost boyishly high; his delightful humour lights up even his philological and metrical disquisitions; be his subject what it may, he always contrived to be witty and entertaining. Only a week or two before his death, that eminently staid and sober journal the *Spectator* made an almost pathetic appeal to him to be dull once in a while, so that people might have more confidence in the soundness of his criticism. One may suspect, however, that Mr. Lowell could not, without doing violence to his own nature, have followed this sagacious counsel. For sagacious it must be reckoned so long as we associate dulness with wisdom, just as we look upon silk hats and umbrellas as guarantees of respectability. Perhaps in time we may learn to distinguish between the grin of vacuity, and that smile playing over the countenance of wisdom which men call humour. Meanwhile, since the gods saw fit to bestow upon Mr. Lowell a plentiful lack of that precious and saving quality of dulness, one may plead on his behalf that there are really so *very* many of us who can be dull all the time without any apparent effort. But Mr. Lowell was not only not dull himself; he hated dulness in others. Towards pretentious ignorance he was mercilessly severe, hardly less so towards learned dulness. No man was so well equipped as he to write a new *Dunciad*, juster and more genial, if less polished, than that of Pope. Perhaps, on the whole, he did not give sufficient credit to learning and industry when these were dissociated —as, unfortunately, they so often are—from wit and brilliance. But if he was as intolerant of Dr. Dryasdust as Carlyle himself, he loved with no common love the masters of the noble English tongue.

As patriotic an American as Mr. Howells, he
did not, like that gentleman, conceive it to be
his duty as a critic to lay violent hands upon the
literary idols of the English-speaking race. On
the contrary, he approached their shrines with a
reverence none the less real because it was never
blind or idolatrous. One cannot help wishing
that in this his example had been laid to heart
by Mr. Howells, who would then have avoided
demonstrating to the world how bad a critic an
excellent novelist may be, if only he set his mind
to it, as Dr. Johnson would have said.

In the matter of style Mr. Lowell falls short of
the chastened perfection of form characteristic
of his friend Hawthorne; one misses in those
brilliant pages of his that subtle aroma of style
which distils from almost every line written by
the author of *The Scarlet Letter*. He is as un-
flaggingly brilliant, almost, as Macaulay, although
his style is by no means so hard, metallic, and
mechanical. Perhaps, after all, the *Spectator* is
right in thinking Mr. Lowell a trifle *too* brilliant;
one prefers the mild and equable light of the
moon to the meteoric glow, the sudden splendours
of the lightning. Dr. Underwood—now alas!
gone, he also—remarks truly that we rarely find
chez Mr. Lowell that 'gracious and serene simplicity' which has so much attraction for us in the

pages of some of the masters of English prose. To turn from Mr. Lowell to such writers as Addison, Thackeray, and Hawthorne is to pass from a gilded saloon, brilliantly lighted, and hung round with mirrors, to a quietly furnished room, in which the colours are toned down and the lights burn low. Mr. Lowell excites and stimulates more than they, but he lacks that indefinable and restful charm with which they lull our tired ears and quiet our restless brains.

The marks of haste, too, are on much that he wrote. For a Professor, his grammar is sometimes astonishingly loose, as when he says, 'Unless like Goethe he is of a singularly uncontemporaneous nature, capable of being *tutta in se romita*, and of running parallel to his time *rather than be* sucked into its current, he will be thwarted into that harmonious development of native force which has so much to do with its steady and successful application'—a sentence for which a schoolboy would taste the rod. Of the famous first line of the *Traveller* he makes nonsense by citing it thus: 'Remote, unfriendly, solitary, slow.'[1] What would Mr. Lowell have said had he caught any one else making two grave blunders in quoting so familiar a line? It would not be easy to defend against the charge of vulgarity

---

[1] 'Remote, unfriended, *melancholy*, slow.'

such a phrase as, 'The true artist in language is never *spotty*'; or against the charge of pedantry the use of such 'fearful wild-fowl' of words as *butyraceous, eocene, paleozoic*.[1] One cannot help thinking that he delights overmuch in figures of speech which are not uniformly felicitous, as this of Dryden : 'He is a prose-writer *with a kind of Æolian attachment*.' The sentence which follows smacks surely of the Professor rather than of the man of letters : 'So powerful is this hallucination, that we can conceive of *festina lente* as the favourite maxim of a Mississippi steamboat captain, and ἄριστον μὲν ὕδωρ cited as conclusive by a gentleman for whom the bottle before him reversed the wonder of the stereoscope, and substituted the Gascon *v* for the *b* in binocular.' The most risible of men could hardly smile at fooling of this sort. A little more of this, and one would suspect that the Rev. Homer Wilbur is not a creation at all, but merely the professional *alter ego* of Mr. Lowell himself.

Lastly, to bring our faultfinding—always an ungracious but sometimes a necessary, task— to an end, the formlessness, the disjointedness of some at least of Mr. Lowell's papers mars our pleasure in the reading. Arnold's habit of choos-

---

[1] '*So few*,' says Mr. Lowell elsewhere, 'has long been denizened.' And when, pray, was *denizened* denizened ?

ing some striking saying, using it as text, and re-
curring to it again and again, savoured, it may
be, of mannerism, and in the end palled upon
one; but at least it gave his essays a coherence
and a unity which are often absent from Mr.
Lowell's efforts in the same sort.

If the form of Mr. Lowell's essays is not absolutely faultless, the substance is almost uniformly
excellent. His critical essays cover a wide field,
although he was not so encyclopædic in his range
as that prince of critics, Sainte-Beuve. Where
all are so good the task of selection is difficult;
but if one wished to give a notion of Mr. Lowell's
critical powers at their best, perhaps no better
choice could be made than the altogether admirable papers on Dante, Chaucer, and Dryden.
The very collocation of these names is itself a
striking testimony to the breadth of Mr. Lowell's
sympathies; a man who can appreciate both
Beatrice and the Wife of Bath has clearly
emancipated himself from the fetters of Puri-
tanism. In the way of vivid and picturesque
description Mr. Lowell has left nothing better
than the picture of Florence and its surroundings
at the opening of his paper on Dante. As befits
a study of such a man, the whole essay is pitched
in a lofty tone. 'Among the statues around the
courtyard of the great Museum at Florence is

one figure before which every scholar, every man
who has been touched by the tragedy of life,
lingers with reverential pity. The haggard cheeks,
the lips clamped together in unfaltering resolve,
the scars of life-long battle, and the brow whose
sharp outline seems the monument of final victory
—this at least is a face which needs no name
beneath it.' This is only one of many singularly
fine passages. Particularly notable also in the
same way is the contrast drawn between Greek
and Christian art, which recalls Ruskin at his
best. Of French literature through all the stages
of its development, from the *Chanson de Roland*
and the *Roman de la Rose* down to Victor Hugo,[1]
Mr. Lowell had made a special study; his knowledge of early French authors was perhaps greater
than that possessed by any other English critic,
and this knowledge he found means of turning
to admirable account in his excellent essay on
Chaucer. Chaucer, with his wide and tolerant
view of human nature, his unique and haunting
melody, his gracious 'worldliness,' his genial temperament, half that of the artist, half of the

---

[1] In one of his latest volumes—that devoted to the early English
dramatists—he institutes a felicitous comparison between Webster
and Victor Hugo, noting in both the same strain of exaggeration,
the same love of strong effects; both, indeed, are giants who, not
content with their natural height, must ever be standing on
tiptoe.

bon vivant, was an especial favourite of Mr. Lowell; indeed, in the essay on Dryden he alludes to him incidentally as 'the greatest but one' of our poets. Surely Mr. Lowell has in this case fallen into the fallacy of the 'historical estimate'; it is hard to believe that he would in all seriousness set Chaucer above Milton. That he was not, however, wholly influenced by the fact of Chaucer's coming so early in English literature is sufficiently proved by the amusing way in which he disposes of poor Gower; it would have been only fair to recognise that Chaucer also has his *longueurs*, although Mr. Lowell would no doubt have admitted this, but retorted that Gower had nothing else. In the same essay one may demur to Mr. Lowell's description of the Anglo-Saxon as 'having no sense whatever, or at best small, of the ideal in him; . . . you shall not find a poet in a hundred thousand square miles — in many prosperous centuries of such.' What Mr. Leslie Stephen calls the 'detestable lay-figure of John Bull'[1] must surely have crossed and obscured Mr. Lowell's usually clear vision when he wrote this. It would certainly be an altogether arbitrary criticism which should attribute all the ideal qualities in Shakespeare, Shelley, Keats, Tenny-

---

[1] *Hours in a Library: Nathaniel Hawthorne.*

son, and the rest to other than Anglo-Saxon influences.

The *Dryden* is a masterpiece ; quite the best thing, it seems to me, which has been written of Glorious John,—luminous, suggestive, sympathetic, teeming with wise and witty observations. Nowhere else has Mr. Lowell shown more thoroughly how he knew

' happily to steer
From grave to gay, from lively to severe.'

'As I read him,' he says of Dryden, 'I cannot help thinking of an ostrich, to be classed with flying things, and capable, what with leap and flap together, of leaving the earth for a longer or shorter space, but loving the open plain, where wing and foot help each other to something that is both flight and run at once.'

Pope naturally follows Dryden, but with him Mr. Lowell is not quite so successful. I do not think his essay will bear comparison with Johnson's *Life*. Despite the fact that the world seems to have tacitly agreed to say of the Doctor, 'Let not his writings be remembered : he was a very great man,'[1] he is really hard to match on his own ground. His vision was clear enough, but he had voluntarily shut himself up in a

[1] ' Let not his frailties be remembered : he was a very great man.'—Johnson on Goldsmith.

dark room, the dark room of eighteenth-century criticism. He was emphatically *not* on his own ground when he essayed to criticise Milton and Shakespeare ; but with Pope he was thoroughly at home, and the result is a remarkable study, in which his incisive and massive common-sense makes up for his lack of imagination. Mr. Lowell, of course, approaches Pope from a different standpoint, and succeeds in saying some admirable things on a subject which might have seemed hopelessly hackneyed. As Dr. Garnett remarks, his strictures on the *Essay on Man* are a little hypercritical ; and, in any case, it seems hardly worth while to go about at this time of day to prove that Pope was not a great reasoner, or a profound philosopher. This, however, is excellently put : ' His more ambitious works may be defined as *careless thinking carefully versified.'* And as an example of concentrated criticism, what could be better than the manner in which he sums up Pope: 'Measured by any high standard of imagination he will be found wanting ; tried by any test of wit he is unrivalled.' We could not give this praise higher in its kind than by saying that it has the crispness, conciseness, and point of one of Pope's own couplets. It would really be impossible in short space to sum up Pope's merits and shortcomings more adequately and more justly. Mr. Lowell's heart, however, was not with Pope and his school, but with the Elizabethan dramatists and their legitimate successors at the close of last century ; his ear was attuned to the 'large utterance of those early gods.' Of Spenser no one has written more charmingly than he. At the close of his critique on the author of the *Faery Queen* he rises into a strain of that fine eloquence of which he was a master, though he used it sparingly. 'Whoever can endure unmixed delight, whoever can tolerate music and painting and poetry all in one, whoever wishes to be rid of thought, and to let the busy anvils of the brain be silent for a time, let him read in the *Faery Queen*. There is the land of pure heart's ease, where no ache or sorrow of spirit can enter.'

It would have seemed impossible to say anything new of Shakespeare, but even in this case Mr. Lowell contrives to make some good points,[1] although the opening statement that 'it may be doubted whether any language be rich enough to

---

[1] He calls the paper *Shakespeare Once More*, as though to suggest that an apology were needed for a new study. Indeed the vitality of Shakespeare is marvellous, considering the freaks of his legion of commentators and critics. One would hardly have been astonished had the patient given up the ghost while the doctors were learnedly discussing his symptoms.

maintain more than one truly great poet' can hardly be regarded as other than a paradox. His remarks on Shakespeare's poetry—that wave of sound breaking into a thousand clear ripples of melody—are admirable, and his analysis of Hamlet's character is subtle and delicate.

The ferocious onslaught on Professor Masson rather takes away from our pleasure in reading Mr. Lowell's *Milton*; his *Wordsworth*, on the other hand, is almost wholly admirable. He pours ridicule on Wordsworth's pompousness, his lack of humour, his frequent lapses into the flattest of prose. He saw clearly that much of what is worst in Wordsworth's poetry resulted from his failure to distinguish between what is *common* and what is merely *commonplace*;[1] while on the other hand, he gave ample recognition to the purity and loftiness of his character, to that magnanimous egotism (if the phrase may be pardoned) in which he resembles Milton, and to the great reform of which he was, if not the originator, at least the first wholly conscious exponent—a reform by which he freed English poetry from the bonds of artifice, informed it with a greater depth of thought, and achieved a new and admirable simplicity of style and diction.

---

[1] A failure which is responsible for Peter Bell and his legitimate descendant, Mrs. Leo Hunter, with her plaintive little lay about *The Expiring Frog*—one of Dickens's happiest touches of satire.

Among still more recent writers Mr. Lowell deals with Carlyle and Swinburne. The *Carlyle* is excellent reading, but has evidently been written under the soreness of feeling caused by Carlyle's description of the Civil War as the smoking of a dirty chimney, and we must agree with Dr. Garnett that 'from the point of view of a purely objective criticism it is much too severe.' Carlyle's influence, both on Mr. Lowell's style and on his thought, was perhaps greater than he was at that time willing to allow; his address on *Democracy* has points of similarity with the great Scotsman's teaching,[1] and in the following sentence from a slashing article on one of the false gods of New England—James Gates Percival —he seems, if I am not mistaken, to have caught the very trick of Carlyle's manner: 'The meaning of which proclamation was essentially this: the vital spirit has long since departed out of this form once so kingly, and the great seal has been in commission long enough; but meanwhile the soul of man, from which all power emanates and to which it reverts, still survives in undiminished royalty; God still survives, little as you gentlemen of the commission seem to be aware of it—nay, may possibly outlive the whole of you, incredible as it may appear.'

[1] But his tone is more optimistic than that of Carlyle.

R

Mr. Swinburne is almost the only living writer criticised in Mr. Lowell's collected works, and to him he is perhaps something less than just. He makes *Atalanta in Calydon* the text for an able and eloquent diatribe against such artificial attempts to bring back the Greek form. We may, however, agree with all that he says on this head, and yet think that Mr. Swinburne works best under the wholesome restraint of classical models; a restraint which seems to curb somewhat that riotous exuberance of diction, and that inveterate abuse of alliteration, which are the radical vices both of his poetry and of his prose. And surely 'graceful' is hardly the word to characterise some at least of the choruses in *Atalanta*: they are nothing short of magnificent.

On Mr. Lowell's excursions into the field of politics I need not dwell at any length. His political attitude is sufficiently indicated in the address on *Democracy* which he delivered at Birmingham, and the lecture on *The Place of the Independent in Politics* reprinted in his *Political Essays*. In the former he sets himself to justify democracy as not only inevitable, but on the whole the only possible scheme of things for present-day needs. 'It is only,' he says pithily, 'when the reasonable and practicable are denied that men demand the unreasonable and impracticable, only when the possible is made difficult that they fancy the impossible to be easy. Fairy tales are made out of the dreams of the poor.' At the same time we may gather from the other essay, as well as from *The Cathedral* and the *Epistle to George William Curtis*, that he had the scholar's love for the goodly heritage of the past, and the natural shrinking of the man of fine culture from the occasional rawness, roughness, and crudity of democracy. His attitude could not perhaps be better described than in the words with which he paints Fitz-Adam :—

> 'A radical in thought, he puffed away
>   With shrewd contempt the dust of usage gray,
>   Yet loathed democracy as one who saw
>   In what he longed to love some vulgar flaw,
>   And, shocked through all his delicate reserves,
>   Remained a Tory by his tastes and nerves.'

Nor was it without some natural misgiving that, proud of the past of his country, and confident in the gloriousness of her future, he contemplated the corruption of American politics. 'Could we only,' he exclaims in bitter irony, 'have a travelling exhibition of our Bosses, and say to the American people, "Behold the shapers of your national destiny !" A single despot would be cheaper, and probably better-looking.' 'Our

leaders,' he asserts, and I am afraid the phenomenon is not confined to America, 'no longer
lead, but are as skilful as Indians in following the
faintest trail of public opinion.'

'What we want is an active class who will
insist, in season and out of season, that we shall
have a country whose greatness is measured, not
only by its square miles, its number of yards
woven, of hogs packed, of bushels of wheat raised;
not only by its skill to feed and clothe the body,
but also by its power to feed and clothe the soul ;
a country which shall be as great morally as it is
materially ; a country whose very name shall not
only, as now it does, stir us as with the sound of
a trumpet, but shall call out all that is best within
us, by offering us the radiant image of something
better and nobler and more enduring than we,
of something that shall fulfil our own thwarted
aspiration, when we are but a handful of forgotten
dust in the soil trodden by a race whom we shall
have helped to make more worthy of their inheritance than we ourselves had the power, I
might almost say the means, to be.'

I must now bring my survey of Mr. Lowell's
works to a close, incomplete on some sides,
inadequate on all, as I feel it to be. The feeling
with which I take my leave of him I am happy
to be able to express in words fitter and more

beautiful than any I could write. In his fine
preface to *Men and Books*, Mr. Robert Louis
Stevenson says of the authors he there deals with
—how admirably, the readers of the volume know:
'These were all men whom, for one reason or
another, I loved; or when I did not love the
men, my love was the greater to their books. I
had read them and lived with them; for months.
they were continually in my thoughts; I seemed
to rejoice in their joys and to sorrow with them
in their griefs; and behold, when I came to
write of them, my tone was sometimes hardly
courteous, and seldom wholly just.'

And so of Mr. Lowell I would say that if the
tone of my imperfect criticism is not one of
unmixed eulogy, if I have had to point—certainly
with no malicious pleasure—to imperfections and
flaws which impair the artistic value of his works,
I would not on that account be thought to hold
his fine gifts lightly, or to be insensible to the
debt of gratitude which I, in common with many
thousand readers, owe to a writer who knew
better than most how to make his readers his
friends and familiars. There are some authors
who seem to hold us at arm's-length, so that we
never feel at ease with them; there are others
whose admirable talents extort our admiration,
but for whom we can feel no personal liking.

Mr. Lowell—need I say it?—belonged to neither of these classes. His large, sunny, and buoyant temperament shines through all his works, and we feel ourselves irresistibly attracted towards a nature so rich, so prodigally gifted, and yet so genial and so humane. An author of whom we may say this may not have set foot upon the topmost peak of Parnassus; his place may not be among that shining and glorious company—so small in number, so diverse in race and gifts—for whom we confidently predict an immortality of renown; perhaps for that very reason he comes closer to us who are not of the eagle kind, and find it hard to breathe for long space the clear and rare ether of those shining heights. And surely he must be accounted both happy and useful in his day and generation to whom men go, as to a dear friend, alike for sage counsel and for cleanly mirth.

THE LIFE AND WRITINGS OF ERASMUS [1]

IN the history of the intellectual development of Europe, the influence of no single man counts for more, perhaps, than that of Erasmus. The distinguishing characteristic of that development has been the constantly increasing distrust and dislike of formulæ which have nothing but tradition to rest upon, the free play of the human mind upon those great problems which were once so arbitrarily disposed of by the mere *ipse dixit* of an infallible church. It is true that the Reformation was the great outward symbol of the breach between the old order and the new, and it is also true that Erasmus held aloof from the Reformation, and viewed its progress with something like dismay. But none the less is it the case that the spirit of free inquiry which culminated in the Reformation was originally set on foot by the writings of Erasmus. Indeed, if he often seems out of tune with his own age,

[1] Gray Trustees Prize Essay, Edinburgh University, 1895.

the reason is that he is speaking to the first half of the sixteenth century with the voice of the latter half of the nineteenth. Erasmus was not, we are often told, a great theologian. Certainly he did not set himself to construct a rigid and well-defined system of theology; but it is precisely because, with a wise and just instinct, he shrank from all rash dogmatism, that he is so significant and attractive a figure in the history of religious thought. In his own day he suffered the usual fate of those who practise the golden mean, and who cultivate that virtue which a modern critic was never tired of recommending under the name of flexibility. The bitterness of partisanship, however, evaporates wonderfully in three centuries; the echoes of the obloquy with which he was once assailed have well-nigh died down, and something like justice can now be done to a man who was certainly not faultless, but who can show so many titles to our sympathy and admiration.

The pathetic story of the sadly chequered lives of the parents of Erasmus has been told by Charles Reade with rich historical colouring and unexcelled imaginative insight. Here we must content ourselves with a very rapid sketch of his youth and early manhood. Born at Rotterdam, probably in 1467, the illegitimate son of Gerard, a native of Tergouw, and Margaret, the daughter of a physician of Siebenburgen, Erasmus was, at the age of thirteen, left an orphan by the death of both his parents. Either through negligence or downright fraud on the part of the guardians the little property which Gerard had left melted away to nothing. To conceal their delinquency they hit upon the plan of forcing Erasmus to enter a monastery. He would then be provided for, and no awkward questions need be asked as to what had become of the funds. But Erasmus was young and ardent. The four years he had spent at the famous school of Deventer had inspired him with an intense passion for learning ; he felt conscious of his powers, and had no liking for the notion of burying his talents and his ambition in a monastery. But his guardians were inexorable; both threats and cajolery were used, and Erasmus at last, feeling his own helplessness, gave way. Two years were wasted in a conventual prepara- tory school at Bois-le-duc, where Erasmus com- plained that he learned nothing, and then he entered upon his novitiate in an Augustinian monastery at Stein. Those who had thus kid- napped him—the phrase is his own—cannot be congratulated on the success of their project. The result was to inspire Erasmus with an undying hatred of monasticism. Alike in playful satires and in serious appeals, he always drew a black picture of the monastic mode of life. From his own account it is abundantly plain that Erasmus in a monastery was like a nightingale in a cage. From the first, literature was the one passion of Erasmus; in his very cradle the Muses had set their kiss upon his forehead. But for letters his companions cared nothing at all; their tastes were coarse and sensual; their conversation disgusting or inane; their religion merely external. The diet of the monastery did not suit his delicate stomach; fasting disagreed with him; he loathed the very smell of fish.

But deliverance seemed hopeless. Once a monk, always a monk—that was the rule. It seemed as though Erasmus were destined to pass his life at Stein; but when he had spent five dreary years there, a fortunate chance opened the prison doors for the unwilling monk. The Bishop of Cambray selected him as his private secretary; the necessary dispensation was granted, and Erasmus left the monastery, never to return.

All along, the darling wish of Erasmus had been to go to a university in order to perfect himself in his studies. After some time the Bishop sent him to Paris, and promised to support him there. Erasmus started full of hopes and rejoicing in his newly-found freedom.

He did not find that Paris was the paradise
which he had thought it from a distance. The
College Montaigu, at which he entered, was one
of the strongholds of the old scholastic theology,
for which, from the first, Erasmus felt a strong
distaste. The discipline was severe, the fare
wretched, the accommodation scarcely decent.
The Bishop proved more liberal of promises than
of gold, and those pecuniary troubles now began
of which we hear to weariness in his early letters.

Erasmus had come to Paris, not only to steep
himself in the culture of the place, but to study
the great book of life. It would seem from his
own confession that he lived in a freer way than
befitted an ordained priest, and possibly some
rumour of this may have reached his patron's
ears. He supplemented his scanty income by
taking private pupils, and by one of these, Lord
Mountjoy, he was invited to England. He gladly
closed with the invitation. Already he felt that
he had exhausted Paris. He was now an accom-
plished Latinist, but tuition in Greek was not to
be had in the city by the Seine, and Erasmus was
casting longing eyes on Italy, the seat of that
New Learning which was arousing Europe from
the sleep of the Middle Ages. But alas! as he
complained, one cannot fly without wings, or
travel without money. In England, however,

Grocyn was teaching at Oxford the Greek he had learned in Italy from Chalcondylas, and to Oxford Erasmus went, probably early in 1498.

This, the first of his many visits to England, may justly be regarded as one of the turning-points in his life. His reputation was as yet a thing of the future; but his urbanity, his genial pleasantry, his sparkling conversation, the wide range of his reading, soon secured him a host of friends. He was charmed with his reception, and wrote with singular and obviously sincere enthusiasm of England and the English. He was fortunate enough to be brought into the closest contact with two of the noblest Englishmen of that or any other age. In Thomas More he found a man of a more transparently honest and ingenuous turn of mind than himself, a man also with a profounder speculative grasp, but with a kindred humour, the same love of fun and sarcasm, the same keen insight into hypocrisy and pretence. Even greater and more far-reaching was the influence exerted on his mind by the character and teaching of John Colet. Erasmus was profoundly touched by the noble simplicity of Colet's life, the masculine strength of his intellect, the ardour and thoroughly practical character of his piety. Colet had been in Italy, but he had altogether escaped the infection of that semi-paganism which in Rome and Florence had accompanied the Revival of Learning. He was now engaged in a serious and noble effort for the purification of religion, by discarding the subtleties of the Schoolmen, and by taking his stand on the simple and historical meaning of the sacred text. The foundations of that vast edifice which had been reared by the subtle intellects of Scotus, Aquinas, and their followers seemed to his practical mind radically unsound, their abstruse speculations so much intellectual effort run to waste. Erasmus eagerly drank in those new opinions, and it is not too much to say that there is hardly one of his books in which we cannot trace the influence of Colet's teaching. The monastic system he had been already taught by bitter experience to rate at its true value, and he was henceforth to be the uncompromising assailant of the obscurantism of the scholastic divines. The warmth with which Erasmus clung to his friends is one of the brightest features of his character, and there are no finer feats in literary portraiture than the admirable sketches he drew of More and Colet, so happily rendered are they, so finely touched, so exquisite, alike in taste and literary grace.

Two years passed pleasantly away in the study of Greek and in theological discussions with

Colet, and then Erasmus took his departure from England (1500). His English friends had generously made up a purse to carry him to Italy, but Henry VII.'s custom-house officers relieved him of these funds at Dover, and Erasmus was forced to return once more to Paris, which he reached broken in health and depressed in spirits. For the next six years he lived mainly at Paris, with frequent visits to Orleans and the Low Countries. He had still a hard fight for a living, but he had found a new patroness in the Marchioness of Vere. Erasmus never affected a mock modesty ; he had a strain of that magnanimous egotism which often goes with the consciousness of high powers, and he was never ashamed to depend on patrons for the means to carry on his work. Although his literary skill and his exquisite humour lend a touch of grace to what might otherwise seem mere abject appeals for money, the picture of him with his hat perpetually in his hand is not a particularly pleasant one to contemplate : one would like if one could to banish that vision of him as a sturdy and persistent beggar. But any outburst of moral indignation would be both unjust and inane. He was, it is true, sometimes forced to flatter, but he never sacrificed his essential independence of thought and speech. It would undoubtedly have

been the nobler course to dispense with the aid of
patrons, and to be content with the garret and
the dry bread of the poor scholar. But if Erasmus
was not a Johnson, neither was he a Swift. He
never put his talents up to public auction; he
merely accepted what was, after all, a far from
adequate recompense for his immense services in
the cause of literature and sound religion. In
more fortunate times for authors his all-sufficient
patron would have been the public; as it was,
Erasmus received less for works which wrought a
moral revolution than a modern writer of a third-
rate novel which has the success of a day.

Soon after his return to Paris Erasmus sent
forth the first of his great books—the *Adagia*. √
The description of this work as a collection of
proverbs and aphorisms is apt to make one conceive a poor opinion of its literary worth. And
certainly in its original form it was nothing more
than a mere compilation. But as edition followed
edition, not merely was its bulk enormously
increased, but Erasmus contrived to introduce
more of his own spirit into the work. He was
quick to seize on the hint for an original disquisition, and the caustic comments on the manners
and vices of the time which were gradually added
are in his most characteristic vein. Here, as elsewhere, he is chiefly preoccupied with the vices

of the Church, and more than once the monks and divines come in for a rough handling. That the *Adagia* answered a real need of the time is sufficiently shown by the constant call for new editions. The Renaissance, in fact, had awakened a lively curiosity regarding the sages and poets of antiquity, but to the great mass of the people the classics were altogether inaccessible. We can therefore easily understand the enthusiasm with which a book giving, in manageable compass, the choice essence of those scarce and coveted volumes was received by a public tired to death of the arid logic of the Schoolmen, and of the insipid literature purveyed by the Church.

To this period also belongs the *Enchiridion* (1501-3). For a devotional book, it lacks warmth and fervour, but its counsels are eminently sound and practical. Written while Erasmus was fresh from his contact with Colet, it shows the impress of his teaching on every page, above all in the slight stress which it lays upon the ceremonial and dogmatic aspects of religion.

After a second short visit to England in 1505, Erasmus at last found himself able to carry out his long-cherished dream of a journey to Italy. Here also disillusionment awaited him. Julius II. the *pontifice terrible* was then Pope, and was ravaging Italy in order to extend his dominions. In nothing was Erasmus more consistent than in his hatred of war, and of Julius he always spoke with extreme abhorrence. The intellectual impulse of the Renaissance had almost died away; '*in Italia*,' wrote Erasmus, with epigrammatic terseness, '*frigent studia, fervent bella*'; and if the moral atmosphere of Rome was not so stifling to him as it was at a later time to Luther, he was not blind to the deep-seated corruption which underlay the fair exterior of a refined and liberal culture. Rome, however, could not but appeal to him on the intellectual side, and the warmth of his own reception predisposed him in its favour. He might possibly have settled down permanently in Italy, but in 1509 great news recalled him to England. Henry VII. was dead, and the partisans of the New Learning conceived great hopes of his young, handsome, and brilliant successor. Erasmus caught the contagious enthusiasm, and hurried back to England, with high anticipations of the honours which awaited him. To beguile the tedium of his journey he meditated his famous satire the *Praise of Folly*, which was put into shape on his arrival, and printed at Paris in 1511.

The *Praise of Folly* ranks among the most famous satires of the world. In this amusing *jeu d'esprit* Folly, in her cap and bells, mounts a rostrum and addresses her votaries—that is to say, all the world. The remark of Dr. Marcus Dods, that Erasmus as a satirist belongs to the school of Lucian and Goldsmith rather than to that of Juvenal and Swift, is true so far as this example of his satire is concerned. It is eminently witty and spirited; Erasmus must have been in one of his most buoyant moods when he composed it. The tone is gay and genial, and the irony is remarkably well sustained throughout. No class of the community escapes a touch of Folly's lash. Hunters, gamblers, merchants, lawyers, poets, grammarians, men of letters—all in their turn are set in a ludicrous light, and are all described as worshippers of Folly. But it is when on the scholastic divines and the monks that Erasmus bears most hardly. Of the Schoolmen he says: 'These men possess so much learning and subtlety that I think even the Apostles themselves would want another spirit if they were compelled to engage in controversy with this new race of divines.' On the monks he is even harder. They are remarkable, he says, only for their dirt, their ignorance, their clownish manners, and their impudence. He then takes a higher flight, and aims his shafts at the luxury of the great dignitaries of the Church, not sparing even the Pope himself. He had not forgotten the scenes he had witnessed in Italy, and the indelible impression they had left on his mind is seen in his unsparing censure of the pomp and magnificence of the Cardinals, and the lust for war and territorial aggrandisement with which that 'decrepit old man,' Pope Julius II., was consumed.

When Erasmus reached England he found Henry VIII. too much absorbed in his warlike designs against France to pay much attention to a mere man of letters. Instead of the rich honours which he had confidently expected, he was forced to content himself with a paltry professorship at Cambridge. As Gibbon puts it in his balanced and antithetical manner: 'Erasmus learned Greek at Oxford to teach it at Cambridge.' His stipend was small; the scholars were few and poor; the society was uncongenial; worst of all, Erasmus could not tolerate the Cambridge beer, and good wine was scarcely to be had. On the whole, Erasmus must have thought with longing and regret of the happy days spent at the sister university on his first visit to England. He was voluble in complaints, and when he received the appointment of councillor to the Archduke Charles, with a pension attached, he gladly left England. For the use of

Charles he wrote the *Institutio Principis Chris-tiani*, a book full of excellent, if somewhat obvious, counsels, and anticipating in some respects the arguments and conclusions of modern political economy.

For some years Erasmus had been engaged on an edition of the New Testament, and the time had now come when this *magnum opus* was to be given to the world. He hurried on to Basle, where Froben had a famous printing - press. Froben received the great scholar with open arms, and a group of earnest and enthusiastic young disciples gathered round Erasmus, and lent him a willing aid in his arduous task. The *Novum Instrumentum* was put hurriedly through the press, and appeared in 1516 with a dedication to Pope Leo.

To understand the full significance of the appearance of the *Instrumentum* requires a strong mental effort. It was the first edition of the Greek text. Hitherto the sole version in use had been the Vulgate, and such was the deplorable ignorance of the common run of ecclesiastics, that they talked as though the Apostles had spoken and written in Latin, or as though the Vulgate had dropped direct from heaven. To alter a single word of the received version seemed to them nothing short of heresy. Before the appearance of the work Erasmus had a foretaste of the puerile sort of criticism he was to expect. Martin Dorpuis addressed to him a letter of strong remonstrance, in which he argued in the most childish fashion for the authority of the Vulgate. 'I adhere,' he wrote, 'to the Latin because I cannot bring myself to believe that the Greek codices are more correct than the Latin.' One may readily imagine the smile of half humorous despair which would rise to the lips of Erasmus when he read this naïve protest.

By the very act, then, of publishing the Greek text Erasmus had taken a bold step forward. But this was not all. To translate the Bible into the common tongue was regarded by ultra-orthodox theologians as a crime for which the fire and the stake were too mild a punishment. The mind of Erasmus revolted at this barbarous notion, and in repudiating it his language took an unusual glow and fire. ' I wish,' he declared, ' that even the most ignorant woman could read the Gospels and the Epistles of St. Paul. . . . I long to see the day when the husbandman shall sing some verses of them as he follows the plough, when the weaver shall hum them as he sits at his shuttle, when the traveller shall while away with their stories the weariness of his journey.' These were, indeed, golden words, and never let us fail to pay a due tribute to Erasmus for his share in making possible the fulfilment of his pious aspiration.

In the *Ratio Veræ Theologiæ*, which was printed with the first edition, Erasmus urged the principles which Colet had laid down in his famous lectures at Oxford. 'Read the Scriptures,' he cried, 'with open eyes; study the history of the times, the character of the writer, and the circumstances of those to whom he wrote. Do not place a blind reliance on the Fathers: the best of them were but men, ignorant of some things, mistaken in others.' Only thus, he urged, could we grasp the real meaning of the sacred text. His object, however, was not so much scholarship as practical piety. The ampler our knowledge, the more vivid would be our realisation of the person and teaching of Christ; and the love and service of Christ was the one great object of the reverent study of the Scriptures.

The practical application of this sound and historical conception was seen in the notes he appended to his work. Again and again he rejected the forced and fantastic interpretations which had become traditional; he strove constantly, with a perfectly open and unbiassed mind, to elicit the real and vital meaning of texts which in the hands of the Schoolmen had become quite unintelligible.   His success was not always perfect, but he took such an immense stride forward, that it is no exaggeration to describe him as the father of modern exegetical science.

Erasmus was now at the zenith of his reputation. He was universally admitted to be the greatest scholar on this side of the Alps.   In Latin he was unrivalled ; Budæus perhaps surpassed him in Greek erudition, but the fame of the Paris *savant* was that of the scholar merely, while Erasmus was a man of letters in the widest sense of the term.   He had done more than any other man in the cause of learning and the *belles-lettres*. By his edition of the New Testament he had justified the hopes that Colet had long ago formed of him.   The dominant scholasticism was reeling under his skilfully aimed blows.   He had contrived to steer an even keel between the Scylla of the semi-paganism of Italy and the Charybdis of the obscurantism of the scholastic divines.   From the pedantry that so often accompanies profound scholarship he was entirely free ; he bore his load of learning lightly, and no man ever knew better how to 'steer from grave to gay, from lively to severe.'   He has often been compared to Voltaire, and certainly the parallel holds so far as the scope and range of their influence are concerned.

Milton prayed for an audience 'fit though few';
Erasmus could count with certainty on having
the whole of Europe for an audience. He had
extricated himself from those pecuniary troubles
which embittered his youth and early manhood.
Popes, kings, and cardinals were all eager to do
him honour. He was in constant correspondence
with the heads of Europe—a fact of which he
boasts with a vanity surely pardonable enough
in one who owed everything to his own genius,
aided by an industry almost unexampled. It
seemed as though he might count on a happy
and peaceful old age, and on being followed to
his grave by the regret of all Europe.

But call no man happy until he is dead. In 1517
the storm of the Reformation broke out, and
henceforth Erasmus lived in an atmosphere of
constant controversy. There can be no doubt
that it was he who had laid the train to which
Luther applied the match; but when the ex-
plosion came no one was more surprised and
dismayed than Erasmus. The keenest observers
often show a lamentable lack of foresight; but
the truth is that Erasmus had been lulled into
a false security by his dream of a peaceful and
gradual reform—a dream of the ivory gate, as
Froude has finely called it. In the light of
subsequent events the hope seems a singularly

futile one. We must remember, however, that the favour with which his own books, with all their plain speaking, had been received by the heads of the Church encouraged the delusive dream that they would of their own accord take up the herculean task of reform. Still, one fact alone might have served to undeceive Erasmus. It was above all on Pope Leo, that indolent and graceful epicurean, that his hopes were fixed, and, by the irony of fate, it was Leo who, by the shameless traffic in indulgences, gave the signal for the strife. The sale of indulgences shocked and scandalised Erasmus ; but ought it not also to have brought home to his mind the truth that corruption had so eaten into the very vitals of the Church that only the knife and cautery could work a cure ?

When the storm burst forth in all its fury Erasmus felt himself to be on the horns of a dilemma. At first he put forth all his efforts to still the tumult. He pressed on both sides the wisdom of moderation. Of Luther personally he spoke with respect, while he disclaimed all connection with his doctrines, and unreservedly condemned what to his cool and critical temperament seemed the Reformer's violence and wrong-headedness. There is something, it must be confessed, a little disingenuous in his repeated protestations that he had not read Luther's books; at all events, the retort was obvious that surely it was his business, as one of the intellectual leaders of Europe, to make himself acquainted with works which were everywhere stirring men's hearts to their depths. But as the strife grew fiercer it became impossible for him to maintain this balancing and neutral attitude. At last he yielded to the pressure put upon him, and, sorely against his will, entered the arena against Luther by the publication in 1523 of his treatise on the *Freedom of the Will.* The book, we need not doubt, represented his sincere convictions, but it does not rank with his best performances. In argument it was wavering and inconclusive, and the coldness of its tone contrasted strangely with the intense and burning ardour of his great opponent. His intervention was in fact a complete failure. He succeeded only in exasperating the Reformers without satisfying the orthodox party. Five years after its appearance, the Paris Sorbonne passed a severe censure on his writings —so little had he gained from joining issue with Luther. At the same time we must dissent from those who look upon his choice of so abstract a subject as an act of intellectual cowardice. Luther himself, it is plain, had no such feeling. He justly enough regarded the theory of the impotence of the human will, with all its corollaries, as the very cornerstone of his system, and he had long been aware that his views were not shared by Erasmus.

The difference between Luther and Erasmus, in truth, went far deeper than can be accounted for by any mere doctrinal disputes : at bottom it sprang from a profound divergence of temperament. Erasmus had a cool and open mind; his horror of strife was so extreme, that he set peace above truth. He had all the humane, but few of the heroic virtues. Between a nature of this sort, and the fiery ardour, the intense moral fervour, of Luther there could be no real agreement. Besides, Erasmus detested dogma, and it was with dismay that he saw Luther pass from attacks on the corruptions of the Church to the construction of a new theology as rigid as the old, though infinitely purer. Fortunately, at this time of day we are not called upon to choose between these two great men. Both had their appointed work to do, and neither could have done the work of the other. If Luther knew best how to minister to the diseased state of the time, it was Erasmus who had first called attention to its ailments.

The incessant controversies in which the Reformation involved Erasmus greatly embittered the last years of his life. Most of these years were spent at Basle, but from 1517 to 1521 he lived at Louvain, and from 1529 to 1535 at Friburg.

Darkness was now closing in around him. He suffered tortures from the stone; like Pope he might have called his life a long disease. One by one his best-loved friends were cut off. Yet such was the buoyancy of his temperament, that into those sad years he compressed what to ordinary men would seem the labour of a life-time. Of his enormous labours in patristic and classical literature, of the host of devotional works which he sent forth, we have no space to speak. His arduous literary toil was continued down to his last hour: when death came in 1536 he was hard at work on an edition of Origen. He made a fruitful excursion into the field of philology by an essay on the right pronunciation of Latin and Greek. Nor had his old lambent humour deserted him. In 1528 he published an exquisitely witty satire on the pedantic imitators of Cicero. By far the most characteristic work of this period, however, was the famous *Colloquies*, and with a short account of this, next to the *Encomium Moriæ*, the most popular of his works, we may fitly bring this study to a close.

The first edition of the *Colloquies* was published in 1519, but like the *Adages* it was long before it took final shape. As Erasmus journeyed hither

and thither over the length and breadth of
Europe, dialogue after dialogue was added.
Sometimes the dialogues were meditated as he
sat in the saddle, and written down when he
reached his inn ; not, however, we may be sure,
till he had his supper and his glass of good wine.
They have a brisk and alert quality that reminds
us of the manner in which they were composed ;
often they are instinct with the bustle and movement of travel in the open air. Erasmus had
travelled over nearly all Western Europe, and
wherever he had gone he had kept both his eyes
and his ears open. He had been brought into
contact with all sorts of men, from emperors and
popes down to drunken bargemen and horse-
cheats. To read the *Colloquies* is to realise that
Erasmus had in great measure the equipment of
the dramatist—the intuitive perception of character, the keen eye for the significant and picturesque detail, the breadth of sympathy, the quick
and eager curiosity. And the result is that they
give us a more spirited and accurate idea of the
actual state of Europe than pages of arid philosophical disquisition could do.

The *Colloquies* are full of plain speaking on the
vices of the time. The satire has as keen and
trenchant an edge as in the *Encomium Moriæ* ;
and it is perhaps all the more effective because

the sneer is often covert, and the vein of scepticism hardly shows beneath the decorous profession of belief. The invocation of the saints, the
folly of pilgrimages, the excessive veneration paid
to relics, the greed and rapacity of the monks,
their immorality and their contempt for learning
—all these topics are touched upon in the happiest
manner of Erasmus. In spite of their tone of
gay banter, the *Colloquies* were full of grave moral
lessons for the men of the time. They did more,
perhaps, to cut the feet from superstition than the
most fiery denunciation could have done. For it
is in the nature of violent invective to provoke
contradiction and reaction, while well-directed
ridicule insensibly saps the foundations of superstition.

ROBERT LOUIS STEVENSON [1]

HE died too soon, who knew so well to live,
That sword-bright spirit, in so frail a sheath.
Not with head bowed beneath the weight of years,
But with fresh laurels clustering on his brow,
He fares to the far country, whence he comes
Never again to charm our ears with speech
Sweeter than honey or the honeycomb.
The fresh fair face of this green earth he loved,
And all the miracles which Nature works
On sea and sky, deep-bosomed woods and fields,
Where midst the corn the flaunting poppy stands,
Had yielded up their secret to his quest.
We mourn for one whose heart beat ever true
To Scotland, loved and left and hungered for,
And most of all our smoke-wreathed, castled city,
The well-loved city of his birth, which lost,
Alas! too soon, her gallant, gracious son.
'No stars,' he said, 'in all the vault of heaven,
To me so lovely as the lamps which shine
In fair Edina's city when the night

[1] Published in *Scots Magazine*, November 1896.

Descends, and high in air the castle lifts
His huge grim mass across a gulf of darkness.'
Pentlands' black slopes and woods of sombre fir
His footsteps knew, and claimed him for their own.
There had he lain and gazed with musing eye,
Gazed on the spires, the labyrinthine lanes,
The houses rising high and quaintly peaked,
Dimly discerned through wreaths of curling smoke.
Such was his vision ; but his thoughts flew far,
And wandered in the realms of old romance—
Realms kingless long, but now their king had
    come.
Scotland he loved ; but she, the austere mother,
Her forehead clouded with eternal wrath,
Her speech bitter, and her unfrequent smiles
Wearing no softness, thrust him forth from home,
To bear an exile's sorrow through the world—
Sorrow time heals not, no, nor troops of friends,
Nor all the bloom and beauty of the world.
For friends are many, but the name of mother
Belongs to one alone ; that title none
Might share with her who travailed for his birth.
And though the gladsome sun looked down on
    him
From skies more fair than ours, and perfumed winds
Wrapt him in softness, and a summer sea
Smiled and made music round his island home,
No power had these upon his present pain,

For still the sweet and bitter thoughts of home
Caught at his heart, and the old longing grew
That she whose eyes first looked in his might
    gaze
Once more upon them, and her arms might clasp
Him to her flinty bosom once again.
And oft in silent watches of the night
His dreams flew homeward, and he saw again
Her face, furrowed and worn and scarred, yet
    bright
To him and lovely, and his lips shaped words
Of tender greeting, and his eyes grew dim
With mists drawn from the secret springs of joy.
But then the dream would pass, and he would
    wake,
And know himself an exile, who should ne'er
See Scotland's shore again, nor see those hills,
Glorious in green and purple, over which
The shifting shadows softly play ; those streams,
Swiftly down-rushing, deep and dark and troubled;
Those mountains, blue, and veiled with clouds of
    mist.
Sickness he knew, and pain and weary days,
And nights of anguish, when it seemed as though
The morn would never come, nor ever sun
Shower gladness on the sorrowing earth again ;
Yet from his lips no peevish murmur broke,
But with a mind elate he drank the cup

T

Proffered by Fate even to the very dregs,
Singing the while in sweet and even key
Of childhood's happy memories and youth's
Glad dreams and fair presages, and the full
And golden hours of ripe and perfect manhood,
Till, brought within the compass of his song,
The many-coloured symphony of life
Rose on men's ears and filled them with delight.
To those clear heights whereon his spirit dwelt
No taint of that sick languor floated up
Which broods so thickly o'er our lower world,
And with its venomed and malignant breath
Poisons the joy of being, and from life
Takes all its natural gladness.   There he dwelt,
And drank deep draughts of the pure mountain
      air,
Mingling his song to every wind that blew,
Feeling the full, resistless tide of joy
Surge through the inmost channels of his heart.
Happy and radiant spirit! that could thus
Transmute to gold the leaden ore of sorrow,
Distil from bitter herbs a draught of joy,
And like a garland wear a crown of thorns.
As some rich-freighted bark, beset by waves
Crested with cruel foam, when clouds lour dark
And all the sky is waste and void of stars,
Undaunted holds her darkling way, and rides
Erect, and to the wished-for haven brings

Her treasure safe through storm and stress of seas,
So through life's storms he passed, with head held
   high
And mind attuned to gladness, and at last
Dropped anchor in the peaceful port of Death.

Printed by T. and A. CONSTABLE, Printers to Her Majesty
at the Edinburgh University Press